A ~~NGER~~
MANAGEMENT

The Essential Guide

Need
— 2 —
Know

Wendy
Sloane

First published in Great Britain in 2010 by
Need2Know
Remus House
Coltsfoot Drive
Peterborough
PE2 9JX
Telephone 01733 898103
Fax 01733 313524
www.need2knowbooks.co.uk
Need2Know is an imprint of Forward Press Ltd.
www.forwardpress.co.uk
SB ISBN 978-1-86144-080-8
Cover photograph: Stockxpert

Contents

Introduction

It's estimated that one in five of us has a problem controlling our anger on a regular basis. So if you find that occasionally tempering your temper is a problem, you're not alone. But if you also look deep inside yourself and discover that your bad moods, aggressive behaviour and perhaps even violent outbursts are starting to have a negative impact on your relationships with friends and family, your self-esteem and even your job, it may be time to get help.

Anger is a natural human emotion, and we all need to get angry from time to time. Some of us, however, find that our blood boils at the slightest irritation, and that we can become incensed and outraged by an incident others would find trivial. If you slam the phone down every time you have a minor spat with the bank, indulge in road rage on a regular basis and more often than not get in a punch-up whenever you have a bit too much to drink down the pub, anger may be getting the best of you.

Anger management is a method by which people of all ages, genders and backgrounds can learn to express their emotions in a positive, beneficial way. It's not about 'controlling' angry emotions; it's about having a balanced and healthy approach towards them. It's about learning how to use assertive communication techniques, and about getting along well with others without offending them or taking away their rights. It's also about learning how to control the physiological feelings that often are accompanying strong emotions – before they get out of hand.

If you wonder if you have an anger problem, take a look inside yourself. Do you regularly have explosive outbursts of negative behaviour that you find impossible to control? Are your relationships characterised by your need to control them, either mentally or even through physical means, such as domestic violence? Do you fly into a rage at home, at work or on the road over relatively minor things? Alcohol or drug dependency may also cover up an anger problem, as well as certain types of depression or anxiety.

Recognising that you have a problem can be frightening at first, but knowing that others before you have made the leap should help you take heart. By reading this book, you are taking the first step towards becoming healthier, stronger and more in control. You will learn not only why you get angry, but also how to stop your emotions from spiralling out of control. You will also learn:

- What triggers your anger.

- Why anger can be so addictive.

- How to distinguish between assertive and aggressive behaviour.

- The importance of recognising anger triggers.

- Ways to de-stress and feel better about yourself.

- Breathing, meditation and other physical techniques to help you cool off.

- Life-affirming steps to help you think more positively.

- How to resolve other issues in your life.

- Toxic anger syndrome (TAS).

- What to do about anger in relationships.

- How to help a friend or family member with an anger problem.

Anger management is a tried and tested way for people to learn how to deal with their tempers, and become more focused, happier and better balanced human beings. The goal is to help reduce the negative emotional and physiological feelings that anger can create, and to learn how to deal with those feelings on a calmer and more positive level.

You may feel after reading this book that you would like to embark on an anger management course, or have therapy to help you resolve underlying issues that contribute to your feelings of anger. It might look like a long hard road, but learning how to recognise your problems, how to express your anger in positive ways and getting further help, if appropriate, is a major step towards becoming the person you want to be.

Only you can create the positive changes you need to feel better about yourself and have others feel better about you. Take the first step today, and read this book. Learn how to control your anger – before it controls you.

Disclaimer

This book is only for general information about anger management and is not intended to replace medical advice although it can be used alongside it. Anyone who suspects they may have anger management issues should contact their GP in the first instance.

Names of all case studies have been changed.

Chapter One

What is Anger?

Anger is one of the most common of human emotions, and perhaps one of the most primitive as well. It can be a good thing – it acts as a signal to tell others when we think their behaviour is out of line, and can be employed as a learning tool to discipline. It is also used as part of the 'fight or flight' response, an innate biological function we use to control stress.

However, when anger routinely tends to get out of control, it can be destructive. It ceases to be helpful or even remotely beneficial, and turns to something that is negative and often even cruel. Perhaps even more importantly, when we use anger as the primary way to deal with everyday situations, it can lead to a range of problems – at home, at work, at school and with friends, family members and lovers.

Why anger management?

Learning to control your anger and use it in a constructive, rather than destructive, way is the crucial aim of anger management. Understanding why you get angry is the first step, as well as how your personal anger manifests itself (which varies greatly from individual to individual). Only when you have a full understanding of your own psychological make-up can you begin to make changes in your behaviour for the better.

With anger management, you can learn to put a lid on violent outbursts, destructive behaviour and passive anger (this last type may not be as noticeable to others, but it still makes you simmer inside). Anger management can help you deal with your everyday stress and recognise the triggers that set you off – and help you avoid them. When you recognise you have a problem and start taking steps to solve it, you're already more than halfway there.

Why we get angry

People get angry for many reasons, and what angers one person may not anger another. In an ideal world, we would only get angry because we are provoked. Unfortunately, for those of us with anger management problems, the littlest thing can 'provoke' us into acting in a negative way, either physically or verbally, which we may later regret.

For most of us, anger is a response to a feeling of unhappiness or loneliness that we feel in our lives. When we have to endure something we don't want to deal with, or would rather avoid, we are made unhappy. Most of us can deal with that – we trip on the carpet and stub our toe, for example, and wait for the pain to subside. But for some of us, it's a fine line between feeling (usually) temporary unhappiness and full-blown anger.

Reasons for outbursts

Experts in human behaviour have been able to pinpoint some primary reasons why we get angry. Some of these reasons are obvious, some are less so. Have a look and see if they pertain to you. They include:

- Personal insult, real or perceived. Has a colleague said nasty things about you to your boss, or has a stranger glanced at you in a way you find insulting?

- Frustration with life or a specific event. Do you have a persistent chip on your shoulder about the way your life has turned out? Or are you angry because you didn't get the pay rise you worked so hard to achieve?

- Threat, real or perceived. If your daughter's boyfriend has made overt comments to you, you may feel yourself getting angry. Or maybe you're a bit paranoid about your next-door neighbour, who you believe is plotting revenge over some long-ago dispute. In reality, he may have forgotten all about it.

- Built-up resentment. Long-term relationships over which we feel we have little or no control can make many of us feel resentful. We can also start to simmer if we feel we're not appreciated enough, either at home or at work.

- Unhappy childhood. Leftover unhappiness from our childhood can leave us feeling powerless, and often we seek to compensate by making ourselves appear bigger than we really are – and that can mean meaner, scarier and angrier.

- Over-inflated ego. Sometimes a good, hard look at ourselves will help us to understand that it's not really all about us – all the time!

Symptoms of anger

Every healthy person gets angry from time to time. However, people who could benefit from anger management are those who often experience the following symptoms, sometimes for no apparent reason whatsoever:

Types of behaviour

- Explosive outbursts that can result in either the destruction of personal possessions or public property.

- Withdrawing socially because of anger.

- Steadfast refusal to complete tasks on time.

- Refusal to follow rules or instructions.

- Always challenging or disrespecting authority, even when there is no need.

- Tendency to complain about authority figures behind their backs.

- Using abusive verbal language on a regular basis.

- Indulging regularly in passive-aggressive behaviour.

- Refusal to take part in specific activities where good behaviour is expected.

- Exaggerated hostility to minor irritants.

- Judging people harshly and unfairly, often with little evidence.

'The proud man hath no God; the envious man hath no neighbour; the angry man hath not himself.'

Joseph Hall, English Bishop, 1574-1656.

Physiological symptoms of anger

People who experience anger on a regular basis may also be aware of a host of physiological symptoms that accompany their emotions. The reason for this is because the brain is the epicentre of all our emotions, and as such releases chemicals to all the organs in our body, chemicals that over time can even cause disease, such as heart disease and stroke.

When we get angry, we experience a chemical reaction in our body. Adrenaline and noradrenaline, commonly known as the stress hormones, are released into the bloodstream. Normally they make our heart beat at a certain rate, but when more and more of them are released, our heart beats faster, our blood pressure soars and our breathing gets faster.

These chemical reactions can be accompanied by a burst of energy that can cause a deficiency of sugar, meaning that we can begin to shake and also to feel a tenseness in our muscles, caused by the 'fight or flight' feeling that is being generated from within.

Thus the most common physiological symptoms of anger can include:

- Shaking or trembling.
- Dizziness which may be accompanied by a feeling of unreality or disequilibrium.
- Grinding or clenching your teeth – often to such a degree that your teeth show permanent damage as a result.
- Reddening of the face.
- Sweating, often this is mainly in the hands.
- Increased or rapid heart rate. Occasionally this occurs to such a degree that you may think you are experiencing a heart attack.
- Headache, stomach ache or both. In some people, other parts of the body are affected as well.

Additional physical symptoms

Some people might experience other symptoms that accompany or precede an angry outburst. Learning to recognise them can help you to better pinpoint when negative behaviour is about to occur and nip it in the bud before it gets out of control.

Types of physical symptoms:

- Uncontrollable desire for a drink, smoke or illegal or prescription drugs to calm down.
- Acting sarcastic or rude.
- Losing your sense of humour.
- Losing your sense of perspective on a situation.
- Acting abusive or abrasive towards others.
- Starting to pace, rub your head, pull your ears or perform another idiosyncratic action.
- Clenching your fists.

Why some people get angrier than others

It's a well-known fact that some people are more prone to lose control than others. By the same token, some people show their anger through outbursts of volatile emotion and then calm down easily, while others never really show how angry they are at all. Instead, they tend to simmer and sulk, and their anger is reflected by their moody and often grumpy behaviour.

It's difficult to pinpoint why some people are easily angered when others aren't. Psychologists, particularly those who believe in behaviour genetics, say it's genetic and that we are born with a predisposition to a specific type of personality. They make reference to babies, some of whom have angelic, happy personalities, while others seem to be born irritable.

Communicating or shouting?

Others, such as those who believe in nurture vs. nature, say that background and upbringing play a larger role. Psychologist Jean Piaget, for example, believed that children construct their own view of the world around them based entirely as a response to their own personal experiences. In families where communication is key and where the channels of discussion are always open, people are less likely to be easily angered. In households where children receive the impression that yelling and shouting is the norm and that chaos prevails, they are more likely to be angry in later life.

Expressions of passive anger

When we can learn to recognise and identify anger before it takes control, it can be easier to rein it in. Sometimes, however, we allow our emotions to bottle up, thus setting a basis for resentment to build and grow. When that happens, the result is often passive anger.

Passive anger can manifest itself in a variety of forms, and how it is expressed depends on the individual. Some people act manipulative and cold, secretly plotting behind their colleagues', friends' or spouses' backs. They are the people who may write poison pen letters, spread rumours and love to gossip.

Pointing the finger

Other people tend to blame themselves for everything, making lots of apologies and inviting criticism. Along with these are those who appear to be more than willing to sacrifice themselves, but who by doing so let everyone know how much they have suffered. They also tend to be ineffectual and/or dispassionate, allowing others to sort things out while they watch from the sidelines.

Finally, people who are passively angry sometimes become obsessive about detail, demanding perfection in everything. Or they may choose to avoid any conflict at all. Instead, they may sit and simmer until everything threatens to boil over – that's when they explode.

Expressions of aggressive anger

Aggressive anger is easier to identify than passive anger, in part because it fits the conventional profile of anger more succinctly. If you tend to lose your temper, fly off the handle or have any type of violent outbursts, chances are your anger is aggressive. The good news is that because aggressive anger is usually more obvious, it's often easier to treat.

People who characterise their anger as being aggressive often get into trouble at work, and also have difficulty maintaining personal relationships, both with friends and at home. Their behaviour can range from intimidation to outright destruction.

Types of aggressive anger

- Threats – these can be as simple as yelling a threat to someone you know, or as complicated as wearing a gang uniform or making veiled jokes.

- Intimidation – at work, rest or play, anything where the end goal is to build you up by making the other person feel small.

- Destruction – this can be destroying yourself through drinking too much or destruction of other people's property.

- Violent outbursts – anything from punching a hole in the wall to domestic violence or beating up strangers.

- Being selfish – not willing to think of anyone beside yourself, even when it comes to people less able than you, such as your children.

- Blaming others – being unwilling to be the culprit for any action, even when it is obviously your fault.

- Acting in a grandiose manner – e.g. driving too fast or spending too much.

'Aggressive anger is easier to identify than passive anger, in part because it fits the conventional profile of anger more succinctly.'

Summing Up

Anger can be used as a positive emotion, but when it is routinely used as a way to control and discipline others, it can be destructive. People who cannot control their anger will eventually face a host of problems in all aspects of their everyday lives, which is why learning to keep control is so vital.

Everyone is different, which is why anger manifests itself differently in different people. It is important that we learn to understand the triggers that can make us angry, and how our anger is manifested, both physiologically and in relation to other people. Some people use expressions of aggressive anger, others are more passive. Either way, feeling consistently angry – and acting on it – will not help resolve the issues that make us angry in the first place.

Anger management has been proven to be an effective way for people seeking to control their anger. Looking for professional solutions to funnel our feelings into different, more creative emotions, as outlined in chapter 8, can help us resolve deeper issues in our own personality which will eventually reflect upon our life as a whole. Through anger management you can learn to control your anger, before it begins to control you.

Chapter Two

Why Anger Gets Out of Control

Everyone gets angry from time to time, which can actually be a healthy response to things which antagonise us. When a child is constantly picked on in school, feelings of anger are normal – it would be considered 'abnormal' if they enjoyed the bullying or found it completely acceptable.

Similarly, how would you feel if your boss was always berating you for things which were not your fault, or patronising you and making you feel incompetent and worthless? In this case, feeling angry – as well as hurt, disillusioned and perhaps even a little bit helpless – is a normal response.

Letting it get the best of you

It's when anger gets out of control, however, that there is a problem. When a child is bullied, he can tell the teacher or stand up for himself by talking back. But if he decides instead to punch his bully in the face and then stomp on his glasses, that's anger getting the best of him.

Similarly, keeping a diary of your boss's unpleasant and unfair treatment of you, and then discreetly reporting his actions to their superior, could be the right thing to do. Taking your anger and resentment home at the end of a working day and venting it on those closest to you, is not.

Anger is an emotion we feel, and it can get transformed into an action. Sometimes, as you probably already know, the action is not a constructive one. It can start off as mild irritation or discomfort, and then quickly flare up into all-out fury and rage.

'I want to be remembered as a great player, but I guess it will be as a player who got angry on a tennis court.'

John McEnroe, former tennis world number one.

When you find yourself more often than not responding aggressively to events – and unable to control how you feel and act – then you know it's time to take action and do something about getting your anger under control.

Recognising the symptoms

Case study

Expressions of anger, naturally, vary from individual to individual – and from event to event. Fifteen-year-old Michael, for example, decided one day that he had taken enough from his little sister, who constantly made him feel that he was nothing more than a source of irritation to her, and that he had no right to be in the family. One day he looked at her and pointed to the kitchen wall. 'Next time, this is going to be your head,' he said, punching an enormous hole in the white plaster.

For some parents, Michael's behaviour is shocking. For other parents, regular outbursts of physical anger from their children may be commonplace, and Michael's behaviour may not even warrant a serious response. So how do we know when our anger is manifested in a normal, constructive way, or when it is destructive and perhaps even verging on the dangerous?

Determining your anger level

The first thing to do is think about what happens when you get angry – and examine how your anger expresses itself. Keep in mind that some people who fly into a rage at the slightest irritation may find it easy to realise they have an anger problem. If you never show your anger but it's constantly eating you up inside and making you feel bitter, resentful and unhappy, you may have an anger problem as well.

Thinking about your anger levels can help you identify what action needs to be taken to keep your anger in control. Do you:

- Slam down the phone when faced with a computerised voice system?

- Have an argument when a stranger takes your parking spot at the supermarket?

- Yell at colleagues or give them the silent treatment when you feel they have usurped your authority?

- Rarely speak to your adolescent child in a normal tone of voice, choosing instead to shout at them for every minor behavioural infraction?

- Get into a rage, with physical symptoms such as teeth-gnashing and fist-clenching, when things don't go your way or when something cannot be accomplished immediately.

Gauging your anger patterns

To learn more about why you get angry, and how to stop the cycle, it's important to closely examine your anger patterns. Few people realise that anger responses can actually become habitual. That means they are a behaviour pattern that we fall into easily without even consciously realising it.

Many of us respond automatically to situations that make us feel stressed and eventually angry without even thinking about it. These descriptions of what can cause anger, and when, might help you see what triggers can set you off.

- Is your anger expressed in a way that tends to overwhelm and surprise both you and others?

- Do you get angry more often, or in a more destructive way, than people you know?

- Have friends, colleagues and family members commented on how often you get angry, or the intensity of your anger?

- Do you feel that your anger occurs a lot more often than is actually necessary?

- Do you use anger to hide your true feelings? In other words, do you find it easier to lash out at someone rather than tell them how you really feel?

'To learn more about why you get angry, and how to stop the cycle, it's important to closely examine your anger patterns.'

- When you get angry, do you find yourself using threatening gestures or unpleasant language towards people?

- Do you use alcohol, drugs or other substances that act on the central nervous system to calm you down when you get really angry?

- Do you often find yourself grinding your teeth, clenching your fists or curling your toes at least several times a day because of anger?

- Can your expression of anger make you seethe and stew for hours, and effectively ruin the rest of the day – for you and/or others?

- Does your anger tend to manifest itself in a physical fashion, meaning that you throw things, hit people, kick furniture etc?

Checklist: how angry are you?

Do you regularly experience some or all of the feelings listed below?

- Anger.

- Annoyance.

- Bitterness.

- Feeling cross.

- Feeling that you've been deceived.

- Disappointment.

- Disillusionment.

- Frustration.

- Furiousness.

- Incensement.

- Indignation.

- Irritation.

- Ill-tempered.

- Livid.

- Rebelliousness.
- Resentfulness,
- Spitefulness.
- Needing to shout.
- Needing to scream.
- Wrathfulness.

Bottling up anger

After looking at the above checklists, you may think you have an anger management problem because so many of the above symptoms apply to you. Think carefully about how often your anger actually manifests itself, and whether or not you need urgent help. If so, talk to your GP as soon as possible.

Some people, however, feel angry all the time, yet never let their emotions show. You might have an anger management problem if you keep valid feelings bottled up inside, which one day may culminate in either a violent outburst or lead to on-going depression and resentment.

Bottling up anger can be destructive on a variety of levels, and can damage relationships seemingly beyond repair. Negative consequences of bottling up anger include:

- Distance in relationships – not showing your true feelings, or being able to talk about them in an appropriate manner, can make you feel distant from people you care about, whether it's your spouse or partner, children or other family members and friends.

- Chronic worry and stress – feeling as if everything is kept on the inside, without ever letting it out, can be a major cause of stress. It takes a lot of energy, both mental and physical, to keep feelings under lock and key. Eventually this can lead to stress exhaustion, including physical symptoms such as headaches, obesity and high blood pressure, as well as negatively affecting relationships at home, work and play.

'Some people feel angry all the time, yet never let their emotions show.'

■ Unhealthy ways of coping – not showing your true feelings to others can lead many people to unhealthy behaviour patterns in their attempts to cope, such as drinking too much, taking illegal drugs or over-eating.

DIY ways of coping

Getting professional help is often the best way of coping with anger problems, as will be explained later in this book. But for people who feel their anger management problems have not yet reached that level, there are many self-help coping mechanisms which can be of great benefit. They include:

■ Exercising regularly – physical activity releases the 'feel-good' hormones we desperately need to feel happy about ourselves and others. Whether you take a regular exercise class, join a salsa dance group or simply go for a regular stroll in your neighbourhood, it's all beneficial.

■ Eating properly – don't underestimate the importance of having a healthy diet. Having a sugar high – and then a sugar low – can play an enormous role in many people's moods.

■ Keeping a diary – writing isn't for everyone, but many people find it an extremely cathartic way of getting their feelings under control. Keeping track of your moods can also help you pinpoint when you get angry and why, and hopefully stave off outbursts or bad feelings in future.

■ Talking to a friend – having someone who understands you well is a gift, and if you have one, why not take advantage of him or her? Often having someone there who really listens and understands is all you'll need to put things into perspective.

■ Listening to music – calming music has been shown to slow down your heart rate and therefore help your entire body to relax.

■ Having a warm bath – not only will you soothe aching, tense muscles but you can also allow your mind to release those nagging, angry thoughts in a warm bath. Make time when you know you won't have any outside interruptions, play some calming music and even light a candle or two.

■ Developing other interests – anger often manifests itself when we feel trapped and therefore resentful. Making the most of your life by developing interests and hobbies is one way to escape from those feelings. Take a foreign language class, visit a museum or go on holiday. It's all about releasing yourself from what you perceive to be the confines of your daily existence.

- Getting a massage – people who have never had a massage before may find the thought of a stranger's hands on their body a little off-putting. But massage is a fantastic way to release built-up tension and stress, and make the entire body relax. And when the body is happy, often the mind follows suit.

Safe breathing exercises

Breathing slowly and deeply can help you calm down, so try these exercises yourself if you feel your anger rising. Make sure you use your diaphragm muscle to get the deepest breaths possible

1. Sit in a comfortable chair or lie down somewhere you feel comfortable, not only physically but emotionally as well. Somewhere quiet will work best.

2. Make sure you are wearing loose clothing, or loosen what you are already wearing.

3. Empty your mind of everything – the idea is to get relaxed – and close your eyes.

4. Place one hand on your chest and put the other on your abdominal area, wherever it feels right for you.

5. Close your mouth and breathe in through your nose. Count to three -- slowly -- as you are doing this.

6. Breathe out slowly, while counting to six in your head.

7. Repeat at least once, or even several times if you feel that will help.

Summing Up

Even though everyone gets angry from time to time, some of us let those feelings of anger – and expressions of that emotion – take over our lives. If you feel that you are experiencing the emotions in the checklist regularly, you should speak to your GP.

To determine what your own expressions of anger are, finding out what sets you off and why is key, as is assessing your own anger patterns. You may find that a little self-help is all the coping mechanism you need. On the other hand, you may decide that professional help is the way to go.

Getting anger under control is achievable, and you have already taken the first step by looking at your anger patterns and manifestations of anger. Congratulations – you are now well on the way to getting your anger in check, and learning better ways of coping.

Chapter Three

Learning Your Anger Triggers

Knowing why you get angry, and what triggers your anger, is one of the most valuable components of learning to manage it. Armed with this knowledge, you can effectively stop those triggers from becoming everyday occurrences, and defuse your anger before it erupts.

Everyone has different anger triggers, which is why recognising what they are can be a bit tricky. But once you acknowledge that certain situations make you more susceptible to giving in to anger, you are well on your way to effective anger management.

Gender differences

According to some people, such as the well-known psychologist Sanda P. Thomas, who has written at length on anger and gender, anger triggers are different in men and in women.

For example, women often get angry when they feel they are being let down by family or friends. They might believe that expectations placed on them by family and friends are unduly high, and that they are not getting anything in return.

A working mum who believes her partner never helps around the house, or a busy stay-at-home mum who gets incensed when she perceives her children treat her as nothing more than a maid. The resentment builds, and unless it is released in proper, constructive ways, it could explode into anger.

Men, on the other hand, tend to get made angry by a complete stranger – or an object. For example, when the television stops working without explanation, or when trying to put flat pack furniture together. Women are less likely to make a big deal out of something they perceive to be relatively remote from them. Instead, they usually direct their anger towards their relationships with others.

Kids get angry too

Small children, for their part, get frustrated – and often angry – when their immediate expectations aren't met. That can be when a toy doesn't work as they want it to, or when they aren't allowed to do what they want. A child's anger is usually an immediate response to a situation, and it can stop abruptly for no apparent reason.

Temper tantrums are a way in which a child shows frustration when they haven't yet developed the skills needed to cope with life. But a child's anger can become a problem if it builds up, or if it manifests itself regularly in a destructive fashion, such as hitting, yelling or biting.

Adolescent anger

Teenagers today have a lot more stresses put on them than teens did in the past. They have to cope with the expectations of home life and school; they have incredible exam pressure as well as constant worries about their future, something many of us didn't have to deal with when we were their age.

Today's adolescents have a lot to contend with. They are coping daily with the hormonal tribulations that accompany puberty and the constant frustration at being treated like children when they feel like adults. But unlike previous generations, they face a lot more exposure to violent and explicit imagery through television and the Internet.

Growing rage

With this background, it's not surprising that many adolescents are struggling to deal with their own feelings of anger and frustration. By the time they begin to enter early adulthood, many are getting more and more enraged with their own lives.

Adolescent anger management may be the next step in helping them deal with their antisocial behaviour, before it spirals out of control. Read more about it and also how the foundations for future anger problems can be set in childhood in chapter 5.

Recognising what makes you angry

A location, situation or even a specific individual can work as an anger trigger. Some people feel angry when forced to do specific tasks at work, others get angry when they come home after a hard day and find complaining children and an exhausted spouse. Still, others find that just talking to that certain someone can put them in a foul mood for the rest of the day.

Keep in mind that what makes one person angry, another individual might laugh or shrug off. Anger triggers vary enormously from person to person. Don't be embarrassed or scared to admit the things that can set you off. Being honest with yourself is enormously important.

Road rage

Road rage is the classic type of situation when we react to an everyday stress with violence or acting out. Experts say that road rage comes about not because we are angry with the driver who cut us off, but because the seeds of rage were planted previously: when you had a fight with your girlfriend or argued with your mum. You are simply acting out your anger at them now, with potentially dangerous consequences.

Everyone gets riled up now and then when driving. Take this test and see if you have real road rage, or if you're just occasionally an angry driver:

▪ Do you ever yell at other drivers – even when they cannot hear you?

- How often do you tailgate the driver in front of you when you're angry?

- Do you often overtake drivers and speed past them because you believe they're not driving fast enough?

- Do you ever threaten other drivers, if only from your car window?

- Do you ever cut people off or perform other dangerous manoeuvres when you believe they're not driving the way you want them to – fast enough, carefully enough, nice enough?

- How often do you try to 'teach other drivers a lesson' to show them you're right and they're wrong?

How did you score? If you answered yes to even one of the above questions, you may have a problem with road rage. If you only yell at drivers when they cannot hear you that is still a potentially dangerous behaviour that could develop into more active expressions of road rage.

Keep an anger journal

'Learning to recognise which situations can set you off is the first step to keeping your anger under control.'

Learning to recognise which situations can set you off is the first step to keeping your anger under control. One way to do that is to make a list or keep a diary of all your anger triggers over the course of a week. Seeing everything laid out before you in black and white can be extremely helpful.

First of all, think about certain emotions you felt just before your anger got the best of you and write them down. They might be quite generalised, or they might be specific to a certain individual or situation. Situations can include:

- Sense of embarrassment.

- Feeling that you are being treated unfairly.

- Having to follow orders, when you think you know better.

- Getting jealous – romantically, professionally etc.

- Strong feeling of indignation, whether warranted or not.

- Inability to do something well and resultant feeling of failure.

- Feeling out of control, helpless.

- Not getting credit for something when you believe credit is due.

- Feeling ignored, overlooked, cast aside.

Specific stressful situations

There are also a host of common situations in which people get angry, although interestingly some people can glide through them without experiencing any anger whatsoever. Look through this list and see if any of these situations would produce feelings of anger in you:

- Poor service in a restaurant.

- Bad drivers.

- Infrequent sexual relations.

- Financial problems.

- Domineering boss.

- Some physical states, such as pre-menstrual tension.

- Being told you have an illness.

- Having to meet a deadline.

Stressful activities

Now, think about some stressful activities which can lead to you feeling unhappy and angry. You're not alone in feeling that way – according to a poll taken by the International Stress Management Association/Royal & Sun Alliance, activities like shopping, paying household bills, going on holiday, housework and being at work are among the most common activities which people in general find the most stressful.

The poll, administered by MORI, interviewed 978 adults working full or part-time throughout the UK. They found overall that almost 60% of these people experienced a 'great deal' or 'fair amount' of stress over the last few years, and that this had worsened in the past year.

Assessing your behaviour

Now that you've written down which situations and anger triggers have set you off recently, ask yourself the following questions:

- What happened right before I got so angry?

- Who was I with when I got angry?

- Did that person say something to set off my anger?

- Where was I when I got so angry?

- When did I get angry – was it right before lunch? Was it when I was tired, late on a Friday afternoon?

Seeing emerging patterns

When you now look through your list, you will hopefully very easily begin to see patterns emerging, which are crucial in helping you understand your anger triggers and why they occur.

Next, you should think about what your reactions were to those triggers. It might be helpful to make a list of five things that really annoy you, or five times in the last week when you got really angry. Ask yourself the following questions about your behaviour at these five points in time. Did you:

- Start an actual physical fight with someone?

- Throw a temper tantrum, with feet stamping and door slamming?

- Throw, break or hit objects, either to demonstrate the intensity of your feelings or because you couldn't help it?

- Use sarcasm, rude words or turns of phrase that you later regretted?

- Yell yourself hoarse?

Looking for another viewpoint

You should be on your way to understanding the situations and triggers that cause your anger and your reactions to them. As a result, you can begin to change your way of thinking. You can take steps to change the way you react to your anger and eventually learn to change your actions as well.

This is something that can be learned and practised until it becomes a natural habit. Here are some tips for learning to look at your anger a bit differently:

- Understand that anger is a choice. You don't have to be angry – you choose to be that way. It is a learned, or an addictive, response to an anger trigger. Learned responses can be unlearned.

- Set the ground rules. If you know your anger tends to spiral out of control, set the ground rules. Next time you meet with an anger trigger, count to 10, go to another room for five minutes or recite the alphabet backwards. Give yourself time to cool off before you act.

- Employ visualisation techniques. Next time you start to get angry, imagine a place where you felt calm, happy and relaxed. This could be a tranquil beach, a peaceful meadow setting, or a childhood holiday where you went on long walks with your family. Allow yourself to think positively, daydream, relax – and get back in control.

- Recognise your internal signs. Next time you feel angry, think about the physical sensations. Do you feel hot, flushed, dizzy or sick to your stomach? Learning your body's seemingly involuntary reactions when you get angry can help you harness those feelings before they spiral out of control.

Anger control

Now, think about how your anger manifested itself. According to anger scholar Charles Spielberger, anger usually does this in one of three ways:

- Outward anger – this type of anger is usually straightforward and directed towards another person or object. It can manifest itself in a variety of ways:

from hitting, kicking or screaming to destroying or harming a piece of furniture or other things. The problem with this anger is that it serves no purpose; instead, it makes things worse and a solution is therefore even further away.

- Inward anger – many people suffer from this, also known as suppressed rage. It's when you bottle up all your feelings inside, until you eventually feel ready to explode. If you internalise all your feelings and rarely let them show, the result can have a knock-on effect on your health, causing you stress in the form of gastrointestinal problems, panic attacks and high blood pressure.

- Control of anger – controlling your anger is what it's all about. This means calming yourself down and giving yourself the space to come up with an action plan that is constructive and results in a real solution. Controlling your anger means reconnecting with family, friends and colleagues, being upfront about what you want and getting your life back on track.

Do you need help?

While anger triggers affect everyone differently, you may need help if any of the following apply to you:

- You are often told to control your angry outbursts.

- You have had frequent run-ins with the law, due to your temper getting out of control.

- You are often involved in squabbles or fights with friends, partners, family members, colleagues and even strangers.

- You sometimes hit your partner or children – or strangers.

- You have been known to lose your temper when you are behind the wheel.

- You have trouble keeping your anger in check.

- You often scream, yell or shout to make your point.

- You use substance or alcohol abuse to deal with your anger.

- You often break things in anger.

- You think you could benefit from anger management help.

Summing Up

Everyone gets angry from time to time, but those who suspect they have a problem should look at what triggers their outbursts. Anger triggers vary from individual to individual, so learning why we get angry can help us on the path towards controlling our behaviour.

While everyone gets angry, some people believe there are marked gender differences between men and women, and how they cope with their own feelings of anger. Children can get angry too, and some adolescents need help in learning how to control their own outbursts, before their behaviour becomes more anti-social.

Writing down what made us angry over the course of a week or two can help us see patterns in our anger. Once we are aware of those patterns, we can begin to do something about them. It's helpful to know why you get angry, what type of people, situations and events make you angry, how you respond when angry and how your behaviour impacts others.

Chapter Four

Deeper Reasons Behind Anger

Anger is a common feeling and a 'normal' emotion. But if your anger is getting out of control on a regular basis, there are probably some deeper reasons that could explain why you have such a short fuse. Understanding what these reasons are can help you better comprehend why you get angry and eventually help you conquer your inappropriate behaviour.

For many people, anger is something they learned in childhood. If, for example, your parents constantly screamed at each other – and at you – and also threw things around the house and slammed doors in an attempt to show their displeasure, you might think this behaviour is normal.

But if you are replicating this behaviour as an adult, with deeply unpleasant consequences, you might begin to realise that other ways of acting are essential. It's never too late to do something about it, so read on to find out how understanding your motives can help you on the path to recovery.

'For every minute you are angry, you lose 60 seconds of happiness.'

Ralph Waldo Emerson, philosopher and poet, 1803-1882.

Is there something behind my anger?

If you have a high level of stress in your life, or experienced traumatic events either in adulthood or as a child, that could be one reason explaining why you feel so angry. While some people can experience several traumas and emerge relatively unscathed, others find adapting to stressful events more difficult, and find their actions – and resultant behaviour – suffer as a result. Anger is just one case in point.

Often, anger is an emotion that's easy to grasp and easy to use, and therefore is something we employ as a cover-up to hide what we truly feel inside. But when anger becomes an automatic or even an addictive response, it's too easy to resort to using it in a variety of situations on a regular basis.

Clues to your emotions

For most people, there are obvious clues to decide whether or not there is a lot more behind feelings of anger than simply being born with a short temper. Some clues are:

- You have difficulty showing your true feelings and emotions: unwillingness to let people know how you really feel or bottling up emotions inside so tightly that they never escape can be incredibly stressful. When it all builds up to boiling point, the anger takes over.

- You are very reluctant to compromise: you may find it incredibly hard to put yourself in someone else's shoes, even if that someone is as close to you as a romantic partner, child or parent. You might remember that as a child the person who always 'won' the argument was the one who fought the most using the loudest voice.

- You always want to win no matter what: it might have started out as a game, but now you might be used to always being the one on top. It's important for you to always be right, even when it comes to things that are incredibly superficial.

- Different opinions seem a personal challenge, or even a personal affront: people who need to feel in control 100% of the time, or those who have a fragile ego, often get angry when someone is not in complete agreement with them.

- You often feel disconnected to the people you care about most: believing that you are just watching the world go by and not fully taking part can be very difficult to cope with, and can bring up feelings of insecurity and sadness which can lead to anger. Often, this feeling of disconnectedness is the result of post-traumatic stress.

Post-traumatic stress and anger

As a child, most of us are taught that our parents will keep us safe from harm. Then an event or incident happens which can change everything, something that overwhelms and frightens us so deeply that we literally never get over it.

Stressful incident or event

Types of incidents could be:

- Fire.
- Car accident.
- Earthquake or other natural disaster.
- Robbery.
- Mugging.
- Personal assault (including sexual abuse).
- Terrorist attack or other man-made disaster.
- Being taken hostage.
- War.
- Death of a parent, close friend, child or lover.
- Diagnosis of life-threatening illness.

Dealing with post-traumatic stress

Some people find after such an event that they are suffering from post-traumatic stress disorder (PTSD). Symptoms can appear within a few days, a few weeks or a few months, although psychologists says they usually appear within six months of the event. They can include:

- Having flashbacks: some people relive the event again and again in their head, or have nightmares that seem eerily realistic. Sometimes certain things can instantly trigger a flashback – to the point where the trigger becomes almost subconscious. If you had a car crash in a snowstorm, for example, then every time it snows you may have a flashback.

- Feelings of numbness: you may feel as if all your emotions have been used up and there is nothing left over. If you feel emotionally numb, it can have an effect on relationships with friends and family.

- Feelings of avoidance: you might start avoiding anything that will make you relive the event, or anything that you could interpret as a potential threat. If you were attacked on a dark road in the early evening, for example, you may avoid going out of doors when the sun goes down.

- Inability to relax: many people feel they have an underlying need to be constantly on guard following a traumatic incident. The perceived necessity to be constantly looking over your shoulder can be extremely wearing.

- Physical symptoms: these are incredibly common, and while they usually subside, in some cases they continue for a long time. They can include headaches, diarrhoea, back pain, muscle pain and stomach aches.

- Anger, either expressed or suppressed, and irritability: you may feel the incident was your fault, and therefore blame yourself, using anger as a cover-up for your true emotions. Then again, you may feel justifiable anger at the perpetrator of the incident, but are unable to do anything about it. If the perpetrator was a parent, teacher or someone you may have to continue having contact with, your anger may build up – especially if you feel you are unable to do anything about the situation.

Loss of personal safety

Post-traumatic stress appears because we are made aware that we are no longer safe, that the world is potentially a dangerous place and that anything can happen. A horrible event can make you aware that one day you will die – and that you could die at any time.

Interestingly, while most people who go through a traumatic event (such as the ones listed opposite) experience some unhappiness as a result, many will come to terms with what has happened relatively quickly.

But about one-third of all people will find they are unable to shake off the symptoms and that they need help. According to psychologists, the more disturbing and/or prolonged an event, the longer it will take for you to recover and move on.

A word about self-harm

Studies have shown that teenagers who self-harm can benefit greatly from anger management. For example, the National Inquiry into Self-Harm, undertaken by the Mental Health Foundation and the Camelot Foundation, recommends that some classroom time should be spent on basic anger management skills, and that alternative ways of expressing anger can be brought up.

Self-harm is defined as people who deliberately physically harm themselves, not to cause death but as a way of relieving anxiety. Self-harming includes cutting, compulsive hair-pulling (trichotillomania), self-poisoning, burning, scalding and head-banging.

The reasons young people self-harm are numerous. More common reasons include:

- Sexual or other physical abuse.
- Low self-esteem.
- Problems with peer group.
- Problems with family members.
- General depression.

It's estimated that about 24,000 teens are admitted into UK hospitals each year because they self-harm, according to the report undertaken by the Mental Health Foundation and the Camelot Foundation. That means in every

'Anyone can become angry – that is easy. But to be angry with the right person, to the right degree, at the right time, for the right purpose, and in the right way – this is not easy.'

Aristotle, philosopher, 384-322 BC.

secondary school classroom, you could have two self-harmers per class. Group and individual therapy can make an enormous difference to people affected.

Anger and stress

Stress can have an incredible impact on how angry people feel and act. What's interesting is that stress – and stressful incidents – affect every individual differently. If someone jumps a queue in a supermarket, for example, you may feel angry and verbally and/or physically threaten them. On the other hand, you may just stand there quietly, realising that their queue-jumping only means that you'll have to wait an extra five minutes.

The degree of anger or stress you experience is linked with your own interpretation of the event. You might feel that a person jumping the queue has no respect for you and threatens your sense of self-worth. Or you might just shrug it off, telling yourself that the person was obviously brought up with no manners. It all comes down to how you perceive the situation, which is why cognitive restructuring, or cognitive behaviour therapy (CBT), is such an important part of anger management.

Innate personality

One thing that is often discounted when it comes to interpreting why we get angry is our own innate personality traits. You might be uncomfortable with change, and feel insecure when you have to move, change jobs or meet new people. You may be ultra-observant and notice things other people don't. Or you may be overly sensitive and take offence when it's often not intended.

Psychologists have classified most people into two distinct personality types: Type A and Type B. Type A people are normally thought to be more prone to anger than Type B. Look at the characteristics and see which personality type best fits you.

Type A personality – you are seen as a go-getter, with drive, energy and the determination to succeed. However, some people may see your competitiveness as a negative characteristic. You don't suffer fools gladly and you like to do things quickly and efficiently. You hate waiting in a queue and place an enormous emphasis on time management. Sometimes you can be perceived as hostile or aggressive, simply because you don't want to spend time waiting for others to catch up with you. Your temper can be quick to flare when things don't go your way.

Type B personality – you are generally more easy-going than people with a Type A personality, although certain traits may overlap. You are easy to get along with, more relaxed and generally more fun to be with in a group. You're not overly aggressive or ambitious; the downside is that people can see you as being less ambitious as well. You lack any sense of urgency when there is a task that needs to be completed, and you can't always be relied on 100% to get things done. Your health is better as you suffer less from Type A health problems, such as coronary heart disease and hypertension, which can be caused by acute stress.

Case study

Christine has been married for almost 15 years and now finds that she and husband Clive constantly bicker over everything: from whose turn it is to take their six-year-old daughter to school to who should wash up after the evening meal.

Recently, Clive has started shouting whenever he needs to make a point which upsets Christine a lot and often results in her getting in a screaming match with their daughter, who has learned very quickly to defend herself and shout back. Christine blames it on the fact that both she and Clive are Type A personalities:

'When I first met Clive I was attracted to him because he always seemed full of energy. He was always the life and soul of the party, and loved being the centre of attention. He has a very loud voice and I loved the fact that you always knew when he was in the room.

'But after 15 years of being together, I'm starting to feel worn-out. We always squabble, and both of us seem to always want to prove we're right. We have started yelling so much that when he walks into a room, I now feel tense and upset, and anything he says sets me off.

'I get really angry whenever I talk to Clive, even on a mundane topic, and I feel he's become my anger trigger. The worst thing is that I know I take it all out on my daughter, who really doesn't deserve any of this. We are becoming an angry family, although I don't really know why except for the fact that we are lively, outgoing and demanding people, which is both good and bad. We need help.

'I have discussed having marriage counselling with Clive and he now seems up for it. I think the way our daughter is acting is making him realise how important getting help is. We are both looking forward to our first session and I am beginning to feel more optimistic. We both want to keep our family together, and I feel this is a strong step in the right direction.'

Summing Up

Sometimes deeper reasons need to be addressed to explain why we feel angry so much of the time. In some cases, the reason is simply that anger is a learned response we picked up from childhood; a behaviour pattern our parents indulged in on a daily basis that we subconsciously choose to emulate.

Other times, however, our anger is the result of too much stress in our lives, or a particularly stressful event that we have not yet come to terms with. People who have PTSD suffer from anger problems.

Our innate personality traits also play a role in why – and to what extent – we get angry. Eager, busy Type A personalities are more prone to outbursts as they like to always be in control of the situation, completing tasks quickly and efficiently. Type B personalities are more relaxed and easy-going, eager to please yet not that bothered when things go wrong.

Chapter Five

Toxic and Chronic Anger

Some people have mild to moderate anger problems, but some of us have anger that is constantly getting in the way of our lives. That's called toxic anger syndrome, or TAS, and describes people who recognise that they actually cannot control the impulse to express their anger, rage and fury.

People who experience toxic anger not only have outbursts of anger from time to time, but they have outbursts which threaten to take over their lives. In many cases, this anger is so uncontrollable that it has irrevocable impact on friendships, relationships and jobs.

People who suffer from TAS may find it hard to hold a job, to have a long-term – or even short-term – relationship, or to even maintain regular contacts with family and friends. In worst case scenarios, someone who suffers from TAS may resort regularly to violence as a way of dealing with life.

'Violence is the last refuge of the incompetent.'

Isaac Asimov, author, 1920-1992.

TAS - impossible to control

People with TAS cannot control the impulse to express their anger. Instead, anger gets the best of them in everyday situations, and they never know what seemingly innocuous event can set them off. TAS can be the most difficult type of anger problem to treat with simple anger management techniques, as people suffering from it can be unpredictable and volatile.

Wondering if you are suffering from TAS? Often, people identified as having it are in the situation where either their boss or partner has said enough is enough, or they have reached the stage where their GP has told them that their anger is having a serious detrimental impact on their health.

Impact on health

Anger-related stress can affect us mentally and physically. Look to see if you have any of these symptoms which could be contributing to your anger levels:

- High blood pressure.
- Coronary heart disease.
- Obesity.
- Migraines and tension headaches.
- Depression.
- Inability to sleep.
- Loss of libido.
- Digestive disorders such as irritable bowel syndrome (IBS).
- Skin disorders such as eczema, shingles or herpes breakouts (while stress cannot cause herpes blisters, once you are infected with the virus, stress can cause the virus to flare up more often).
- Back problems and chronic pain.
- Over-reaction to everyday events.

Typical TAS scenario

Mike Fisher, head of the British Association of Anger Management (BAAM), admits he wrestles with anger management problems himself. He describes a typical situation, as seen through the eyes of an individual with TAS:

'I am in a supermarket and somebody drives over my foot with a heavy trolley. That is what is known as the activator. The behaviour is absolute fury and indignation. The coping strategy should be "hey, don't take it personally, they didn't mean to do that, maybe they are having a tough day, and perhaps I could be more aware next time." But if you are as angry as me, all you want to do is tear their heart out and shove it down their throat.'

The six golden rules

Mike has six rules he follows when it comes to managing chronic anger. 'All I have to do is remember these six rules and not think about the trigger, the behaviour or the consequences. They always work – if you follow them,' he says. They are:

- Stop, think, take a look at the big picture.
- It's okay to have a different opinion.
- Use your anger journal (see chapter 3).
- Listen.
- Use your support network (see below).
- Don't take anything personally.
- Let go of your expectations.

Support network

Anger management classes usually rely on support networks to help tame anger, and nowhere is this more important than with people who have TAS. For details of national or local support groups in your area, contact the British Association of Anger Management on 0845 1300 286 or visit www.angermanage.co.uk.

Stop playing the victim

Another way to keep any type of anger in control is to stop perceiving yourself as the victim. Often, when tempers flare and things get overheated, it is tempting to think of yourself as the victim. After all, if the fault doesn't lie with you, then why should you have to solve it?

Unfortunately, that type of thinking does more harm than good. While it is all too easy to be influenced by other people's behaviour – and all too easy to be seduced into thinking their behaviour affects you more than it actually does – you need to control your own situation.

Case study

Guy, who was diagnosed with TAS himself, describes a typical day before he sought help:

'I would have a really challenging day in the office. My boss would be dumping all that anger and frustration on me, and in general making me miserable. Usually what I would do is take that anger, misery and frustration home, and dump it on my wife and kids.

'The challenge was before I got home, to call someone and unload, to get rid of those toxic feelings before I unleashed them on my family. I wanted to talk about them.

'I want to do it differently this time, so I speak to the person enrolled in helping me with my anger management. I unload on them so I don't unload on my family.

'That shows how my anger management group is working really effectively.'

That means thinking of yourself in a positive light. Sufferers commonly have poor self-esteem and little confidence – do you want to see yourself that way? Take responsibility for your own actions and realise that you DO have a say in what you do, how you act, and yes, even how others treat you.

Chronic anger

Do you wake up feeling angry, or does your anger sit with you for a prolonged period of time? If so, you may be suffering from chronic anger, which is different from 'normal' anger as it is often there even when unprovoked. This type of anger can be detrimental in many ways, the least of which is that it can ruin the quality of your life.

Checklist: are you chronically angry?

Ask yourself the following questions, and see how many apply to you:

▪ Does the anger stay with you, day after day?

▪ Does talking with certain people, or about certain events or situations, bring up angry feelings?

▪ Can you often feel anger when there apparently is no 'trigger'?

▪ Do you alienate people because they are afraid of your outbursts?

▪ Are people often careful about what they say around you, for fear you'll explode?

▪ Have you ever hurt yourself with your angry feelings?

▪ Has anyone ever told you that you have anger issues?

Effects of angry outbursts

You may tell yourself that nobody really notices your outbursts, and that they are largely under control. But if you take a long, hard look at yourself – and your actions – you may find this is not the case. Chronic anger can have lasting negative effects on an individual and the people around them.

Here are problems which may be affecting you if you are chronically angry:

▪ Ill health – high blood pressure, heath problems, stroke.

▪ Bad performance at work – even if you are doing well at your job, your perception of how you are doing – and your enjoyment – could well be affected.

▪ Mental health problems – you may suffer from insomnia, panic disorder and/ or depression; you might have an alcohol or substance abuse problem.

▪ Family breakdown – your romantic and platonic relationships probably are suffering if you find it hard to let go of your anger.

▪ Feeling of numbness – many people who experience chronic anger have disassociated themselves from their feelings, and go through life without enjoying all the pleasures this world has to offer. It's a way of protecting themselves from feeling too much – except, of course, anger.

Look for triggers

If you are prone to chronic anger, there are some physical states which can set off, or trigger, your aggressive behaviour. Being aware of them can help you control your behaviour better. They are:

■ Hunger.

■ Being drunk or under the influence of drugs.

■ Having a compulsion to do something, such as binge-eating, binge-drinking or having sex with strangers.

■ Fatigue.

■ Sexual frustration.

■ Being ill.

■ Chronic pain.

A chronically angry child

As mentioned in chapter 3, children are only human and also can get angry from time to time. Sometimes, however, it appears evident to either parents, teachers or both that a child is having trouble expressing his or her feelings, or is getting uncontrollably angry on a regular basis. Sometimes the child could benefit from counselling, in particular anger management counselling, or in other cases it may be the sign of a developmental problem such as autism.

Outbursts, temper tantrums, angry flare-ups and even hitting, biting and kicking are all considered normal behaviour for a small child. But if your child is doing some of the following on a regular basis, you may want to sit up and take notice.

Your child may be chronically angry if they are regularly:

■ Destroying their possessions.

- Destroying other people's possessions or property.
- Physically harming their body on a regular basis.
- Threatening to harm others (but more than just, 'If you do that, I'll hit you.').
- Picking up or threatening to use dangerous objects.

Seek help

Some children have difficulties communicating for a variety of reasons, including speech impediments, speech delay or autism. When this happens, they can get frustrated and angry.

But other children may be angry for other reasons – unhappy homelife, violence at home, perhaps they have witnessed a crime or something very upsetting. Sometimes, being chronically angry is a sign that they have a mental health condition or a developmental delay that has not been diagnosed. If you are worried in any way about your child's health, you should talk to your GP, who will organise a referral to get the correct diagnosis and help.

Adolescents can also have anger problems. All too often we tend to skim over this, as we tend to look at adolescence as a time when teens and even some pre-teens are 'supposed' to be angry and questioning the world. If you are worried about your teenager's anger issues, speak to your GP.

Anger management for children

Anger management classes for children can be very beneficial. They will learn:

- New ways to cope and deal with their anger.
- How to reduce the incidence of getting angry in the first place.
- Ways to improve their self-esteem.
- How to deal with stress without getting angry.

It is hoped that some form of anger management education may soon be introduced into the National Curriculum.

Summing Up

Everyone gets angry from time to time, but if you have difficulty controlling your regular feelings of rage and fury you could be suffering from TAS. This syndrome describes people who are flying off the handle on a regular basis and have come to realise that their relationships, jobs and even their health may be at stake.

Adults are not the only ones who suffer from TAS. Children can be affected as well. There are some tell-tale signs that your child may have a problem, either an anger management problem or a developmental disability. If your child shows some of these signs, he or she may need professional help.

Adolescents can also be angry for a variety of reasons. Chronically angry teenagers can grow up to become chronically angry adults. If you are worried about your child or teenager, it's best to take action now – before the problem gets any worse. The same is true for adults, who need to learn effective ways to cope, how to stop playing the role of victim and which type of stress-relieving techniques work well for them.

Chapter Six

Anger and Relationships

Anger can be particularly destructive when it comes to relationships. And that doesn't mean just romantic relationships; anger can also have a negative, detrimental effect on friendships, relationships between colleagues and family dynamics as a whole.

When we live or work in close contact with each other, or simply choose to spend a lot of time in each other's company, we begin to become aware of each other's peculiarities and bad habits. It's easy to start nit-picking at each other and constantly finding fault – and it can be hard to break the cycle.

Squabbling and bickering as a couple

Many couples bicker with each other, and some relationships almost seem to thrive on a bit of banter. But love will eventually wither away and die if a couple argue constantly, whether they squabble about trivial matters such as whose turn it is to empty the dishwasher, or more serious matters such as finances, child-rearing and sex.

A typical cycle consists of a couple having a row, eventually calming down and things going back to normal. But then the cycle begins again. And again. And again. In time, one or both partners will have had enough. It's hard to keep an interest in a relationship when it is choked by anger and frustration.

Ongoing anger can hurt

Ongoing anger, no matter what the cause, can have a hugely detrimental effect on a relationship. When unresolved, it can lead to physical distance and sexual problems. Constant feelings of anger affect not only our relationships, but also our health and our self-esteem.

'My father was predisposed to drunken rages. I would hide under the bed. My sister and I were talking just the other day about the terror a drunken man in a rage can create in a child.'

Antonia Villaraigosa, Mayor of Los Angeles.

Breaking the cycle

Think of your relationship with your partner as a meal. When the meal is over and everyone is satisfied, it's time to clear away the dirty dishes. It's not worth waiting a day, a week or a month until they accumulate almost to the ceiling. You'd then have to live in a filthy mess, and the task of clearing-up that awaits you would appear insurmountable.

When it comes to close one-on-one relationships, it's important to clear away the dishes – or at least the air – as soon as anger rears its ugly head. When you are distressed or unhappy about something to do with your partner, don't wait until it builds up – and then explode. Instead, try talking about problems when they first appear – in a gentle, non-accusatory manner that shows you want things to work, not to worsen.

Couples counselling can help

Often professional counselling can to help bring a couple closer together, resolving the situation and encouraging respect in the relationship. The charity Relate offer relationship counselling services throughout the UK (see help list). If anger issues are more deeply rooted, one partner may benefit from anger management classes.

Living with an angry partner

If your partner seems to be constantly angry, there may be underlying issues – particularly resentments – which are to blame. Holding on to negative emotions such as bitterness, resentment and anger can not only damage your relationship, but your self-esteem and eventually your entire outlook on life. Letting go is vital.

It's important to try to ascertain why your partner is feeling so angry and resentful. Possible reasons could include:

■ A shock – your partner might be feeling angry because you have done something that has hurt them in the past, such as an affair, and they are unwilling to let it go.

- A physical cause – your partner may be pregnant, or coping with a mental or physical illness. They may expect a lot more from you and feel let down.

- Their past – your partner could still be reeling from incidents that happened years ago, such as sexual abuse as a child, a rape or an unhappy childhood in general.

- Your actions – if you did something deliberately wrong, your partner might not be able to forgive and forget.

- Repeat scenario – if something keeps on happening again and again, your partner's feelings of unhappiness and frustration may build up until they are unable to cope.

- Lost dreams – your partner may be stuck in a dead-end job or similar situation and blames you for their own unhappiness with their lot in life.

A word about domestic violence

While anger management is a tool which many different types of people can benefit from, simple anger management classes are not appropriate for people dealing with domestic violence issues. In fact, many psychologists say that confusing the two has led to deadly consequences.

Deb Nagle is a survivor of domestic violence, who has written a book called *Family Terror* (available at www.familyterror.com). 'If you have ever been a victim of domestic violence you know this [needing a simple anger management class] is not the case. The abuser does not lose control of his temper. He plans the abuse in advance, plain and simple.

'He deliberately brainwashes his victim and the abuse evolves from nearly nothing to becoming worse with each incident. It truly is a crime as it is intentional harm to another human being.

'Anger management indeed is not what is needed for these abusers. It has become the socially acceptable thing [to say]: "the judge just ordered me to anger management", meaning I really did not do anything that was really wrong, past losing my temper.'

© Deb Nagle, *Family Terror,* www.familyterror.com.

Anger at work

Some psychologists believe that (limited) anger at work can actually help you move up the career ladder, meaning anger that results in you doing something constructive and productive. A study conducted by the Harvard Medical School, the Harvard Study of Adult Development, says that people should learn how to not suppress their anger but harness it. It goes on to say that repressing frustration or bottling up emotions is not the way forward, as negative emotions can help us to focus our attention on important issues. Outright fury was detrimental, however, especially in a working environment.

'We all feel anger, but individuals who learn how to express their anger while avoiding the explosive and self-destructive consequences of unbridled fury have achieved something incredibly powerful in terms of overall emotional growth and mental health,' said Professor George Vaillant, leading author of the study. 'If we can define and harness those skills, we can use them to achieve great things.'

'For most people, approximately one-third of their lives is spent working with people not of their own choosing.'

Managing workplace anger

Most people, however, agree that anger at work is largely destructive. Whether it's directed toward your boss, your other colleagues or inwardly toward yourself, anger rarely leads to a positive conclusion.

In fact, a recent US Gallup poll said that one in every five American workers had been angry enough to hurt another co-worker in the last six months. However, the vast majority of anger problems in the workplace can be dealt with competently and adroitly, before they ever reach that level.

Irritating colleagues

For most people, approximately one-third of their lives is spent with people not of their own choosing, i.e. in the workplace. Add to that working under the pressure of high demands and increasing competition, coupled with the occurrence of firings and redundancies, and you've got a recipe for disaster. But it needn't be that way.

Everyone has a colleague who rubs them the wrong way, whether it's someone from accounts who is always chewing gum, or an overly ambitious team member that you work alongside. You should resist the urge to voice your anger in an uncontrolled outburst directed at the colleague.

If you have an irritating colleague, don't get mad – get constructive. Here are some sound strategies to effectively deal with colleagues in the office. Once you learn how to handle them, they might be on your side.

Checklist: learn to get along

▪ Decide what the problem is – if they just have an irritating way about them, e.g. too much dandruff, foul breath, they stand too close – then you should try to get over it. If it's more serious and directed explicitly towards you, it's time to take action.

▪ Invite them for a chat – ask them out for a drink and discuss the problem openly. Work together to plan a solution that works for both of you. It might mean agreeing not to work together, if possible, or to stay out of each other's way.

▪ If all else fails, appeal to the boss – if you are positive that someone is stabbing you in the back or stealing your ideas, don't plan retribution or lose your cool, speak to an appropriate supervisor. If you are being bullied or discriminated against, do this immediately – don't try to handle it on your own.

Remember, it's up to you to make the situation better – and that can only be achieved by remaining in control and not letting your temper get the best of you. It's important to defuse situations before they blow up – and backfire.

Take action with your boss

If you have a boss with anger management problems – one who has frequent outbursts – keep the following suggestions in mind:

▪ Don't downplay their anger – when they are venting their rage, you may be tempted to say 'Why are you so upset?' Instead, say: 'I can see you are very upset,' or 'I understand that this has made you very angry'.

- Don't mimic their actions – if your boss starts yelling and shouting, don't yell and shout back, therefore escalating the situation. Instead, stay calm and wait for them to cool down.

- Change your own attitude – it's important to understand that your boss vents his or her rage on other employees because of their own personal anger issues. Don't take it personally, although it may seem an impossible feat, and don't rise to the bait. Although it might feel like it at the time, it's not really your problem. Stay as detached as possible.

- Take notes – if your boss's outbursts persist, take notes and document their bad behaviour. It will help you down the line if your job is ever in jeopardy because of them, and will help you to realise fully the extent of their explosions. It might be better than you think.

Dealing with angry friends

All friendships have their ups and downs. You might have a good friend who is angry at you for a specific reason, either a perceived problem or a real one. Or you may have a friend who is angry all the time, someone you believe needs help before their anger issues begin to get the best of them.

So what can you do if you suspect a friend has an anger management problem? Obviously, you will need to tread carefully and not be confrontational. Here are some tips to dealing with them in an effective, gentle manner:

- Choose a time when they are relaxed and not overly stressed.

- Pick a place that is comfortable and private.

- Explain how their reactions to certain situations make you – and others – feel uncomfortable.

- Give them an example, such as: 'When I told you that John had won the bid for the project instead of us, you yelled and called me a liar. Then you refused to speak to me for the next three days.'

- Ask if they are aware of how they make others feel. If they say yes, discuss it. If they say no, don't attempt to make them see your point.

- Break off the conversation on a positive note and try to talk to them again another time.

- Don't attempt to discuss the problem with other people in attendance; this could be seen as ganging up against an individual and could backfire.

Summing Up

Anger is an emotion that can disrupt a relationship. It can flare up at home, in the office or among friends. Sometimes couples get used to bickering and squabbling as a regular way of expressing their everyday emotions, but pent-up anger can wreck their relationship and cause much distress.

Breaking the cycle is important. Sometimes couples counselling can work, sometimes one or both partners could benefit from anger management classes. You will need to decide together which route is best for you to take.

Anger can also greatly affect people at work, whether it's having to deal with irritating colleagues on a daily basis, or putting up with a bully boss. Sometimes the best approach is to understand that their peculiarities shouldn't affect you and, at other times, confronting the person in a non-aggressive way can work wonders.

Chapter Seven

Managing Your Anger

Many of us find ourselves in situations that can potentially make us angry every day. But it's how we react to those situations or scenarios that determines whether or not we have an anger management problem.

When you feel as if you're about to blow your fuse, controlling your temper can be difficult. That's why learning how to stave off outbursts before they take over is the key to anger management. Being aware of the practical skills needed to keep your moods and thus behaviour on an even keel is what it's all about.

Learning to blow off steam

There are many things you can do to calm yourself down when you feel an impending outburst coming on. Here are some top tips to teach you how to get your anger under control. For some people with mild anger problems, this approach may be all you need.

- Count to 10 – don't act on a whim; instead take a few seconds to calm down. You may realise that things are not as bad as they might first appear, and it will save you from going overboard with anger.

- Give yourself some space – sometimes you might need to divorce yourself from the situation, if only for a few minutes, to collect your thoughts and get your feelings back in control. If you are showing physical symptoms such as clenched fists and heavy breathing, this is especially important. Just walk away – to another room or another part of your home or office. Continue things when you are in a calmer frame of mind.

'Anger is a momentary madness, so control your passion or it will control you.'

G M Trevelyan, historian, 1876-1962.

- Think before you speak – if you need to speak to a boss or a family member about something important, it can be better to write down what you want to say before you say it. That way you avoid flying off the handle and blurting out something you'll later regret.

- Describe the problem using 'I' sentences – in an argument, all too often the common human response is to lay blame. These can range from 'Why didn't you tell me the phone call was for me?' to 'Why are you always so stupid?' It's better to say, 'I'm disappointed that you didn't tell me about the phone call.' That type of language, without laying blame or being too critical, is much more productive in the long run.

- Identify a real solution – don't just think about what made you angry in the first place. Learn how to separate your emotions from the issue at hand, and work on finding a real solution to the problem.

- Don't hold grudges – it can be tempting to hold a grudge and think back on past perceived issues. If your partner is angry because you haven't done your share of the housework and you remember that he or she didn't do his share last week, it's easy to throw that back in their face. Don't. Expecting people to behave in certain ways that conform to your own attitudes and expectations is unrealistic. Forgive and forget will get you further.

'How we perceive things is how things are. While this might sound like an empty truism, it's actually very close to reality.'

Cognitive restructuring: changing the way you think

How we perceive things is how things are. While this might sound like an empty truism, it's actually very close to reality. Changing the way you think about things can change your whole outlook on life, and change the way you react to events, people or attitudes which in the past have made you angry.

The premise behind cognitive restructuring is that we often use colourful words or actions, or indulge in certain types of behaviour, which reflect the inner turmoil ranging inside us. How you think to yourself, for example, often reflects how you see things, whether your perception corresponds to reality or not.

So instead of thinking 'Life is horrible, everything is ruined, things are horrific', put a different spin on things. Think to yourself: 'Things may look bad now, but there's a reason for it. It's not all doom and gloom, and flying off the handle about it won't accomplish anything positive at all.'

Remember also that thinking negative thoughts, and thus using negative and often humiliating words, will only alienate people around you – the same people who, when seen in a different light, can actually help you think of a solution to the problem at hand.

Cognitive restructuring is a more structured approach to changing the way you think, a form of psychotherapy based on the idea that how we think influences our behaviour. It is very helpful in treating people with moderate to severe anger management problems (see chapter 5).

Assertive vs aggressive behaviour

Many of us still make the classic mistake of confusing assertive behaviour with aggressive behaviour. Yet there is a way of getting what you want without resorting to aggression. In Britain, there is a cultural attitude that making a scene or 'creating a fuss' is not the way to go. But if you do it in a way that's firm and fair, without getting angry, it can work.

Psychologists have grouped people's behaviour into four distinct models. Have a look and see which model fits you best at the moment, and which one you would eventually like to emulate.

▪ Passive behaviour – also known as submissive behaviour, this lets other people take control to the extent where your own needs, wants and desires are completely overlooked. You are a shrinking violet and often take the blame for things which had nothing to do with you, although you might be smouldering inside. Traditional gender roles encourage women to be more passive than men.

▪ Aggressive behaviour – openly angry, often with a physical component. You want to stand up for yourself, but you don't care if this means stepping on other people's toes in the process. Aggressive body language and actions accompany this behaviour which assumes that you are superior to others in some way. You can be hostile, blame or threaten others and are rude and sarcastic when you are acting aggressive. Often men are more aggressive than women as traditional gender roles can encourage actions that fit some of these behaviour patterns.

- Indirect behaviour – you are often afraid to talk openly about your feelings, even when it comes to anger, so you employ small child tactics to get what you want. This can involve everything from slamming a door in the middle of a conversation to gossiping. This type of behaviour is often seen as being manipulative as you use indirect means to achieve your goals.

- Assertive behaviour – using clear and direct communication, you only use anger when it takes other people's feelings into account, not purely as a way to lash out and stretch your muscles. You express your feelings openly and honestly and have learned how to say 'no' to unfair requests or demands – without insulting the other person. In a nutshell, you stick up for yourself in an elegant and constructive fashion, and encourage others to do the same.

Letting go of anger as an addiction

Often there is an ingrained pattern we follow when it comes to reacting to negative situations. If you are used to yelling at your spouse every time he or she does something that displeases you – no matter how trivial – that is probably how things will continue. Unless you break the cycle.

Typical pattern

Addiction to anger can happen for a variety of reasons. Usually the cycle begins because you're just not feeling the way you think you should. Perhaps your needs aren't being met, either professionally or personally. You might be feeling abused, neglected or taken advantage of. Nothing feels right, and before too long the anxiety and pain builds up. You don't tell anyone, but you feel as if you're about to explode.

When you do explode, someone gets hurt – either a colleague, your child or your partner. You might feel bad about it, but the initial feeling is that you blew off steam – and the pressure was relieved, if only for a moment.

Is an anger management course for you?

Case study

About a year after Jessica moved in with her boyfriend Dave, the relationship quickly became very tense. They both thought she was largely to blame, so when Dave suggested Jessica take a series of 10 anger management classes, she agreed.

'I was often very irritable and stressed, which showed itself in being short and a bit snappy. I think I have a flash flaring-up temper, which luckily doesn't flare all that often. But I was feeling worried that I was responsible for the loss of warmth and spontaneity in our relationship, and Dave persuaded me that I had an anger management problem. The course seemed a good idea.

'The very first activity was a questionnaire to place all members of the group on a continuum of anger – what we were feeling and how we handled those feelings. I was in a group with people who had a far greater anger management problem than I did, people whose loss of control could regularly result in aggression and violence against themselves and others. Nevertheless, I am very glad indeed that I took the course.

'It helped me to recognise the symptoms of growing emotional pressure. I would typically clench my fists and/or my jaw as irritation started to mount. Before becoming aware of these warning signs, I didn't realise I was feeling so pressurised until my stress and annoyance had built up quite a lot.

'Learning to recognise and take control of anger is like learning to drive. At the start, everything seems to rush towards you very quickly – there's no time to take avoiding action. The more you recognise what stimuli are out there and strategies for dealing with them, the more time you buy to make decisions and act smoothly.

'I remember a guy in the group saying, "There's no time to do anything differently. It's like a red flash and I just lose it…" Over the weeks, we all started to become much more aware of our triggers (what made us angry), our physical state and what to do when we felt a problem building.

'The course gave me a framework of ideas in which to understand my behaviour, time to reflect on my behaviour and choose ways of being more effective, and to practise techniques to prevent or deal with anger problems. I also learned how to be more assertive – I was really, really unassertive, even when I thought I was being quite tough. The supportive feedback from the group helped to correct my misconceptions.

'Now, I try to avoid getting into an anger-provoking situation in the first place. If it is unavoidable, I try to regulate my breathing and resist the temptation to interrupt or speak over someone else, even if they are annoying me intensely. Staying calm and being polite is so much more effective in the long run – and you avoid lots of problems and regrets. If I can make space between myself and the stressful situation, in a controlled way, I will.'

Your outburst of anger felt good, although now you have to mop up the consequences. In fact, it felt so good that you (perhaps subconsciously) want to repeat the experience again and again. But there is a better way of dealing with these feelings.

Summing Up

For some people who only experience minor anger management problems, simple learned actions can help them cope. Counting to 10 before acting on impulse, learning to blow off steam in constructive ways and not holding grudges are all ways you can learn to become less angry. Once you practise these types of actions on a regular basis, they become automatic.

Cognitive restructuring can also help, or learning to change the way you perceive things. Often it's how we see and react to an event that's the problem, not the actual events themselves. Letting go of anger as an addiction is also important; having a temper tantrum can often calm us down afterwards, which is one reason many of us seek to have tantrums in the first place.

Finally, a more structured anger management course can be another way of dealing with outbursts, teaching us to remain calm in potential anger-provoking situations and avoid seeking them out in the first place. Anger management classes also can help you realise that you're not the only person with an anger problem, and that it can be dealt with successfully to help you get your emotions back on track.

Chapter Eight

Getting Professional Help

If your anger management problem is consistently bothering you, or if friends, family and/or colleagues have commented on your temper, it may be time to look into professional help. Often, people are embarrassed by the thought of seeing a counsellor or taking part in a mental health course. Don't be. Getting help is one step towards getting better.

Several types of help are available, but what works well for one person may not work well for another, so it's worth investigating what's on offer before making a decision about what to do.

Statistics on getting help

The UK Mental Health Organisation launched a report in 2008 called *Boiling Point*, which talked in part about the difficulty in getting help for anger management problems.

Key findings included:

- 84% of people polled strongly agreed or agreed that people should be encouraged to seek help if they have problems with anger.

- 58% of the people polled admitted that they wouldn't know where to seek help if they needed help with an anger problem.

- Fewer than one in seven (13%) of people who said they had trouble controlling their anger sought help for their anger problems.

- Those who sought help were most likely to do so from a health professional (such as a counsellor, therapist, GP or nurse), rather than from friends and family, social workers, employers or voluntary organisations.

'When angry, count to ten before you speak. If very angry, count to one hundred.'

Thomas Jefferson, third president of the United States, 1743-1826.

- GPs reported they had fewer options for referring people who had anger management problems, but that classes were available, including those that were privately funded, those run by voluntary organisations and by the NHS.

This is just a short summary – to read the full report, go to www.mentalhealth.org.uk and click on 'campaigns', 'anger and mental health' and then 'boiling point report.' Here you will find the option to download the report.

Seeing your GP

Your GP should be your first port of call. It might be embarrassing at first to discuss things openly, but it's an important step in the right direction. Your GP can suggest tried-and-tested ways for you to deal with your anger yourself if you feel you have minor issues, or they may refer you on for further counselling and support.

While NHS-funded anger management courses are available, as well as those funded by voluntary organisations, you may have to go on a waiting list. If you feel you cannot wait, you may be offered counselling through someone in the GP practice, or you may decide to contact someone privately. If you decide to take the private route, only see a counsellor who is registered with a professional organisation, such as the British Association for Counselling and Psychotherapy (see help list for details).

If your anger issue involves violence, you may be referred to a domestic violence programme which can be a long-term course of treatment. It is important that you let your GP know if you believe your anger issues could be causing a physical threat to yourself or to others.

Anger management classes

Anger management classes are usually held in a group setting, their aim being to come up with effective coping patterns instead of resorting to anger. Classes will help you to transform your anger into healthy actions, such as:

- Assertiveness instead of aggression.
- Problem-solving.

- Finding solutions.
- Empathy.
- Compassion instead of blame.
- Forgiveness.

For more information about classes, contact the British Association of Anger Management (BAAM) – see help list. It also offers bespoke one-to-one counselling for stressed, angry individuals 'across the age and social sphere'.

Group therapy

You might benefit from simply talking to others in the same position and learning to understand your triggers and actions. Paula Hole co-facilitates a therapeutic 11-week course at Plymouth and District Mind called 'Exploring Your Anger'. It is open to anyone who feels they have issues with their anger and the way in which they express it. It works through self-referral only.

'Often, people have very, very painful emotions – they know they feel bad but are not always aware of what emotion they are feeling,' says Paula. 'Often anger is an emotion that is more accessible to them; they can use anger when they are feeling bad but cannot look at an underlying emotion that is far more painful.'

The course is designed to help people become aware of the four core emotions: anger, happiness, sadness and fear; to understand how each emotion makes them feel physically and emotionally, and to be able to differentiate between them.

Paula says 'we then help them to identify triggers for their particular anger, and then look at what life defences or coping strategies are in place already. The defences may be outdated, no longer useful and even damaging to the person now.'

'So we then do a big piece of work where each member of the course looks at a time when they have become angry and things have not turned out how they wished them to. In doing so we help them to identify times leading up their angry outbursts, so they can learn how to make choices to do things differently.

'Very often people say they have no control, that they lose it and see red. That puts them in a place of powerlessness. What we help each person to do is to identify what is leading up to that, to see the warning signs both physical and emotional before they lose control.'

Paula Hole, Plymouth and District Mind, www.plymouthmind.org.uk.

'Very often people say they have no control, that they lose it and see red. That puts them in a place of powerlessness. What we help each person do is to identify what is leading up to that, to see the warning signs, both physical and emotional, before they lose control. We also do an anger impact scale at the beginning and end of the course. We then meet up again in three months, so in effect we are monitoring them over six months.'

For more information, Plymouth and District Mind's contact details can be found in the help list.

Cognitive behaviour therapy (CBT)

CBT is a form of psychotherapy that works on the premise that your own distorted beliefs and thoughts contribute almost entirely to distorted actions and behaviour. Once you control the way you think, you can learn to control the way you act.

Automatic but inaccurate thoughts can contribute to a variety of negative behaviour patterns, such as anxiety and over-eating as well as expressed anger. When you learn to become aware of your thoughts more accurately and realistically, you learn to control your behaviour better.

This is done through therapy sessions which allow you to explore often difficult and painful emotions. The sessions can be difficult but very worthwhile; the coping skills you learn will not only help with controlling your anger, but can help you in a variety of other situations in the future as well.

ABC approach

The ABC approach which is used in CBT is especially helpful when it comes to anger management. It asks you to record – and then view – events in a certain way:

- **A**ctivating event – can also be described as the trigger.
- **B**eliefs – or what happens to you when the event is activated, in other words, what you think and feel.
- **C**onsequences of the event – how you act as a result of the event.

Here is an example using the ABC approach:

- **A** – my boss asks me to finish a project by Friday.
- **B** – she must think I am slacking off, otherwise she would not have given me a deadline.
- **C** – I feel irritated, annoyed and angry, and as a result I go home and yell at my wife.

Using the ABC model, you look back at your actions to see if they are justified, then make practical decisions so that in future you will react to a similar event in a more constructive way.

Not for toxic anger

Mike Fisher, who runs the BAAM, warns that CBT is not usually effective for people with serious anger problems, and recommends anger management classes instead.

'CBT is very generic, covering all bases using the ABC model. People who are chronically angry don't benefit from that. While CBT can be good for individuals with mild to moderate anger problems, anger management is better for those with what we call the toxic anger syndrome.'

Neurolinguistic programming (NLP)

NLP is often used as an anger management technique. While the name may sound a bit complicated, it's actually quite simple. In a nutshell, NLP works on the basis that our reality is the way we perceive things (filtered and interpreted by our minds).

With this in mind, it uses techniques – sometimes in the form of individual therapy sessions with a neurolinguistic practitioner and sometimes in the form of group courses and seminars – to change the way we look at things, and therefore change our behaviour and actions.

As the name suggests, NLP encompasses three main elements:

- Neurology – how our bodies function, how we process the world around us.

- Language – how we interface or react to ourselves and others. In other words, the personal meaning we give to our everyday consciousness and awareness of things.

- Programming – types of world models we create within ourselves. In other words, how we process what we see in the world around us and how we react to what we process.

Hypnotherapy

Hypnotherapy, often combined with NLP, is another popular anger management method. It works on the idea that it helps you control your anger subconsciously, which can be a very effective way as it works from the inside out.

During hypnotherapy, you are induced into a trance-like state where you can discover subconscious reasons behind your anger problem, while at the same time helping make changes in your behaviour. Along with helping you to uncover the deep-set reasons behind your anger, hypnotherapists help you learn your anger triggers and come up with techniques to cope with them.

Some people still think of hypnosis as akin to getting into a trance and clucking like a chicken. The reality is far from that. When you are in a relaxed, comfortable state, and therefore highly susceptible to suggestion, your hypnotherapist will help you solve problems and develop better ways of coping.

Keep in mind that no hypnotherapist can make you do things with which you are not comfortable. Instead, they are simply tapping into your subconscious mind to get the best from you.

Methods of self-hypnosis

Self-hypnosis can also help, especially when it comes to controlling anger. Many relaxation tapes and CDs are available that can help you relax and remove yourself from angry thoughts and feelings. Look online or ask a qualified hypnotherapist to recommend one that could be useful to you. Many qualified hypnotherapists have their own CDs which are available for purchase.

Case study

Karen, 34, runs a media company in London. She had suffered from anger-related issues from as far back as she could remember. Even as a child she would suddenly explode and demonstrate questionable and verbally aggressive behaviour to anyone – and everyone – in arm's reach.

She recalled how her circle of friends was forever changing, both lovers and friends. They were simply not prepared to tolerate her angry behaviour, especially when often it concerned such trivial matters as not wanting to go to a club after having been out for dinner.

Having set up a successful business after graduating, Karen employed a team of 10. But again, the turnover of staff was pretty high. One minute she was the life and soul of the agency, being kind and funny – the next she was lashing out at employees, threatening to sack them, being abusive and often hurling things across the room such as mobile phones and watches.

There was one incident when a member of staff handed in their notice due to personal reasons. Karen's response was to yell out a string of swear words as she clenched her fists and kicked the water urn over.

Having observed her behaviour both in public and private, a worried friend and colleague knew she had to seek professional help. Refusing counselling, Karen agreed to see Monica Black – a master clinical hypnotherapist and NLP practitioner who had previously worked with similar cases.

Monica explains: 'Self-awareness is a key element for anger management because the use of anger management skills presupposes that you know when you are angry and recognise that anger as a cue that something is wrong.'

'However, anger is a learned response, and the anger response can be unlearned through hypnotherapy. There is nothing wrong with occasional, moderate anger. It creates no lasting harm. But chronic, sustained anger can be harmful to both you and those around you.'

In Karen's case, Monica used CBT, the most common approach today for the treatment of problematic anger. CBT embraces control which requires a separation of the person from the emotion, and sets up an oppositional relationship between the client and his or her anger. It helps people to recognise negative thoughts before they become internalised as negative emotions.

Monica taught Karen how to bring down her level of anger in a negative situation. Once this anger was released, it was much easier to control it. Monica also uncovered the reason for the anger – mainly it was due to insecurity and jealously.

As a child, Karen was constantly told she wasn't good enough. This resulted in insecurities around herself and her actions to which she over reacted with angry rages. However, with CBT, Karen learned to understand her anger, release it and eventually keep it under control.

Monica's top tips

Here are Monica's own tips for dealing with anger:

- Don't choose to express your anger in negative ways. That means you should never choose to deal with things in a fashion that can harm you or your relationships with others. Examples include holding a grudge, scheming revenge, blaming yourself for things which are not your fault, drinking to excess or using illegal drugs.

- Know your own anger triggers, and consciously plan how to avoid them. If you are aware of the things that make you angry, you will be more able to stay clear (see chapter 4).

- Create 'break states'. Once you feel that anger creeping up on you, plan a different way to cope – or to escape. That can mean going to the gym, watching a happy film, leaving the room, listening to a happy song or talking to someone who can calm you down.

- Give yourself time to allow the angry period to pass. Once you recognise an anger trigger, know how to deal with it. Ask yourself if the problem will still be bothering you tomorrow, a week from today or next month.

- Use your imagination to create good scenarios. You know how you usually respond to an anger trigger, now imagine yourself doing something else. Instead of venting and telling, visualise yourself calmly walking away, picking up a good book and losing yourself in another world.

Summing Up

Statistics have shown that people are angry – and getting angrier – a survey of 2,000 people from the Mental Health Foundation discovered that Britons are 'more angry than ever'. Yet not everyone is aware of where they need to go for help, or what type of help is on offer. If you feel you could benefit from getting professional help to assist you in controlling your anger, there's no need to feel embarrassed. Anger management classes, cognitive behaviour therapy, hypnosis – there are many types of help available. You can ask your GP for a referral and take the first step towards taking control of your behaviour.

Chapter Nine

Cleansing Out Your Life

Once we realise what our anger triggers are, it's time to take a deep, hard look at our own lives. Often, there are people, situations or events which annoy, irritate or bother us no end. Shedding anger means having the courage to cleanse from our lives things we consider toxic.

It might sound simple, but think about certain people, places and/or situations which always get you all worked up – and angry. You might get incredibly irritated/annoyed/stressed out every year when you have to attend several work-related Christmas parties in a row, or when your in-laws come over to stay with you for three weeks. You might resent having to listen to your cousin talking about her failed relationships all the time, or having to pretend you like a certain type of food to avoid offending a relative. Then again, driving to work every day during rush hour might put you in the foulest of moods.

Some people are just angry, full stop. But if you can identify what makes you angry, who makes you angry and why you are angry, you may be able to take steps to cleanse those toxic situations from your life – and be less angry!

A new lifestyle

Sometimes we need to cleanse our lifestyles to make us happier and more content. We all know about how dangerous it is to put something toxic into your body. Whether it's eating a diet that is high in sugar and fat, drinking to excess or taking dangerous drugs, it all builds up and has a toxic effect on the way we look and feel.

Unfortunately, many of us do nothing about it until we have a nasty wake-up call. That can range from a suspected heart attack, to waking up one morning in a stranger's bed with no recollection of the night before. When that happens, it's usually time to take a good look at the situation and do something about it.

> 'Man must evolve for all human conflict a method which rejects revenge, aggression, and retaliation.'
>
> Martin Luther King Jr, leader of the civil rights movement, 1929-1968.

When it comes to toxic friends, however, we are less likely to dump them than we are to dump the cigarettes and fatty fast food. A toxic friend can be an anger trigger – they may make you feel enraged for specific reasons, or just because they are the way they are. Too often we blame ourselves for a poor relationship, saying that if we were only nicer, more understanding or a better person in general then we'd get along better with someone, be it a neighbour, friend or partner. If your friendship is becoming much more of a bother than a blessing, stop it now.

Recognising a toxic friend

The first step is to identify people in your life you consider toxic. Here are some signs that a 'friend' may not be doing you any favours. They include:

'When it comes to toxic friends, however, we are less likely to dump them than we are to dump the cigarettes and fatty fast food.'

- Being too needy – asking for favours all the time, making others feel guilty when they don't phone often enough, and getting angry if they discover that an event has been held without them – not just a huge party, but even a coffee morning for two.

- Being blunt – always saying what's on their mind without taking the time to put things delicately. Always acting like they always know what's best for everyone and not wanting to listen to any alternative points of view.

- Losing friends quickly – although perhaps making new ones easily as well. Always seem to offend people, or always getting offended by others.

- Constantly interfering in friends' lives, assuming they always know better – wanting to take control because they assume their way is the best, even when it comes to personal issues like romances or children.

- Being incredibly insecure – making up for poor self-esteem by tending to boast a lot, making others feel inferior. In a similar vein, being reluctant to praise or congratulate others for their accomplishments, as it will detract from their own.

- Always quick to anger and often blowing up when things don't go to plan – liking to be in control of things and resenting others taking the lead.

Breaking off the relationship

The next step is to break off the relationship – in an assertive manner. There are three main anger styles:

- Passive-aggressive – doing nothing until the resentment builds and builds, then exploding.

- Aggressive-aggressive – always having an incredibly short fuse, constantly exploding and getting things done in a volatile, unpleasant manner.

- Assertive – standing up for yourself in a constructive, problem-solving way.

Be assertive

According to Mike Fisher, head of BAAM, dumping a toxic friend should require assertiveness, more than anything else. He says:

'What you are describing in relation to toxic friends is about being assertive, knowing what your boundaries are, and starting from the perspective of how you feel. You should say "When you speak to me like this I feel..." or "I feel angry, sad, hurt and scared when you are constantly criticising my relationship with my husband, and actually what I need from you is some support." It's all about being able to communicate clearly your feelings before they start becoming defensive.

Don't over-identify

'Then the challenge, of course, is not to over-identify with how they are feeling. Usually you think "I am afraid to express my thoughts to you as you might become angry, hurt or scared. I don't want to over-identify with how you feel, because when someone criticises me I know how it makes me feel, I feel very ashamed and angry. When I over-identify with the other person it makes it difficult to communicate how I feel, so I have to be sensitive to over-identifying with them, which can create more frustration and resentment with the position I find myself in."'

However, Mike is first to admit that usually people don't do anything when it comes to breaking off a friendship – instead, they just stop answering phone calls or making the effort to keep up the contact. 'The challenge is to actually move beyond that, to dis-identify with them and be explicit.

'Say, "Look, under the circumstances I don't think this friendship of ours is getting anywhere. I have reached out for support and all I have is criticism, for example. I really have thought long and hard about my friendship with you, I feel I no longer want to continue with it."'

Playing the game

'Speak when you are angry and you will make the best speech you will ever regret.'

Ambrose Bierce, journalist and satirist, 1842-1914.

While the above advice sounds great, it's a fact that sometimes, as much as we want to, we cannot dump everyone who makes our lives more difficult. For example, in-laws, difficult siblings and other long-term relationships that are unlikely to change.

If you have to deal with someone who is raising your blood to boiling point, here are a few tips to keep those angry flashes under control:

- Walk away – don't think that leaving a fight means you are automatically the loser. Walking away from something silly makes you the winner. Congratulations for having the courage to extricate yourself from a pointless situation before it gets out of hand.

- Communicate – talk with the person with whom you are having problems, but try to stay neutral. Don't start sentences with the accusatory 'you', try 'I felt sad when the holiday was cancelled', instead of, 'You cancelled the holiday because you don't care about me'.

- Step back, look and listen – often, especially when arguing with someone you have argued with hundreds of times before, such as a spouse, it's easy to fall into those same old patterns of accusation and retaliation. Instead, listen to what they have to say and try to see things from something other than your own viewpoint.

- Forgive – this may sound impossible, but take a moment to think about it. You are angry at your enemies, because that's what having an enemy is all about. If your enemy is no longer a rival in your life, what happens to the anger? It disappears as well. Being able to forgive is hugely important when it comes to letting go of anger.

The clearing process

According to Mike Fisher, another way of dealing with people with whom you are forced to remain in contact is what is known as the 'clearing process'. This is a way of confronting people in a non-threatening, calm and upfront manner, and getting into a helpful dialogue.

Remember that when you are very angry it is virtually impossible to enter into the clearing process.

Choose a moment when both you and the other person are in a calm frame of mind, and when both of you have time to spare and clear the air.

Option one

The first version of the clearing process is as follows:

- Ask the person for 15 minutes of their time.

- Tell them you'd like them just to listen and provide feedback at the end.

- Give them the facts, e.g. 'You said you would help me with my project and then you refused.'

- Tell them your opinion of the situation, e.g. 'I feel as if you have shown that my work doesn't matter to you at all.'

- Tell them how this affected your feelings, and what you want from them in future, e.g. 'In future, I would like you to help me after you promised to do so.'

- Then tell them how you have done the same thing in the past, e.g. 'Sometimes I also forget to carry out my promises and let people down.'

- Then explain how the experience has helped you learn about them and you, how you now understand how you project issues onto them which are not entirely fair and how the whole episode has helped you become more understanding.

- Finally, ask for feedback if warranted.

Option two

This version of the clearing process is for people who are defensive or insecure.

- I feel...angry/disappointed/upset with you.

- Because...you never help me cook/show an interest in my work/say nice things to me.

- When...I was little my dad never helped my mum/took an interest in my mum/was nice to my mum, and this brings up unpleasant memories.

- What I want is...for you to help me/show an active interest in my work/be nice to me without me having to nag you all the time.

- What I am willing to own up about my own behaviour is...although I talk the talk, I don't always do what I promise to do either.

For more of Mike's advice, read his book *Beating Anger: The eight-point plan for coping with rage* (Rider Books).

Dealing with toxic feelings

Like toxic friends, toxic emotions can often play havoc on our bodies – and affect our self-esteem and general health as well. You can repress or suppress toxic emotions, but often if you have an anger management problem you probably choose to express them openly in a way that is detrimental to everyone around you. What can you do?

Well, taking control of toxic feelings often means avoiding situations where those feelings will be reinforced or encouraged to come to the surface. And if you worry that opting out is a cop-out, it's not. It's a coping mechanism that will help you keep your cool and feel empowered.

Summing Up

Sometimes we can get rid of some of our anger by getting rid of the exact cause. If a friend, colleague, activity or specific situation is making you angry, being assertive can cleanse that trigger from your life – in a positive, constructive way.

Recognising what type of relationship is toxic is one way we can start the cleansing process. Once you have identified who they are and how they trigger your negative response, it's important to express your own needs without over-identifying with them. Sometimes it is possible to clear the air with a specific person over specific events, in other cases you might want to stop seeing that friend or stop taking part in a specific event, if all it, or they, do is make you angry.

Opting out is not always a cop-out. Sometimes removing yourself from the situation is the best way to put a lid on the anger you feel, especially if other ways of coping have failed.

Chapter Ten

Staying on Track

Anger is a learned behaviour, and hopefully this book has taught you that there are better ways to express yourself than venting your rage, fury and frustration. You may choose to enrol in an anger management class, have one-on-one therapy, try out hypnosis sessions or simply practise self-help techniques to cool you down.

Effective anger management can help you recognise the frustrations, or anger triggers, in your life and deal with them in a positive, non-confrontational way. Learning about your own anger will put you on the path to dealing with emotions and resolving issues in a straightforward manner that allows you to keep calm and in control.

If you have other mental health conditions such as depression or addiction, you must seek professional treatment – see your GP in the first instance. But don't expect to do everything at once, getting healthy can take time and requires serious concentration and effort on your part – but it's definitely worth it!

'Anger is not a necessary emotion to feel – you can control it and decide to react with another more positive emotion instead.'

Dan Fallon, health promotion and wellness consultant, CIGNA Corporation.

What anger management teaches

Once you have completed your chosen anger management approach, the skills you learn will help you to stay on track, In particular, you should learn how to:

- Identify and recognise the situations that make you angry, and learn how to respond to them in an assertive and non-aggressive way.

- Be able to call on specific skills to calm you down in a potentially explosive situation, such as breathing exercises, removing yourself from the situation and counting to 10.

- Be able to recognise when you aren't perceiving a situation realistically, and change your thinking to reflect what is actually going on, instead of what you perceive to be going on.

- Focus on problem-solving instead of dwelling on your feelings of frustration which can lead to anger, and even fury.

Long-term results

Soon you'll find that being able to increase the possibility of managing your anger will have far-reaching results that can help you in your everyday life, and greatly improve your relationships with people.

Improving your ability to keep your anger under control has a range of benefits – for you, your family and the people you are in contact with on a daily basis. Now that you are working to get your own anger under control, you'll soon be able to:

- Argue less often – anger often results in petty squabbles and bickering, which has a huge impact on the quality of your life. Anger management can help you enjoy better communication with the people you care about most. It will also help you to resist the urge to blurt out petty, rude or hurtful things to people, and stop the damaging effect on relationships that those words can cause.

- Avoid addictive behaviour – people who are chronically angry resort to many different types of addictive behaviour in a quest to fill the void. Whether you have taken comfort or escape in food, alcohol, drugs or sex, you can hopefully stop this now and look towards a better future.

- Feel less frustrated – this is partly because you won't feel you have to keep a lid on your feelings, and people around you will no longer feel as if they are walking on egg shells in order to not upset you.

- Enjoy better health – your overall physical state will improve because you won't have built-up frustration and stress taking a toll on you physically, and you'll have fewer psychological problems as well, such as feelings of chronic irritability and/or depression.

- Be more productive – redirect your energy into more active/creative pastimes.
- Re-build broken bridges – many of us regret things we have said in anger and seek to mend relationships with people whom our behaviour has alienated in the past. Now's your chance.

Assertive, not aggressive

Remember that once your anger is in control you still have the right to be angry on occasion, just not to express it in a negative, damaging or generally non-constructive way. By now you have learned the difference between being aggressive and being assertive. Assertive people have the right to:

- Express their own feelings and let others express theirs.
- Be treated with respect and treat others the same way.
- Tell people clearly and effectively what their needs and wants are, but to also listen to others when they express their own needs.
- To say yes or no without others making the decision for them, and without feeling guilty.
- To not depend on other people's opinions for approval.
- To not make their own self-esteem and confidence depend on others' actions and opinions.
- To change his or her mind.
- To speak up when they don't understand something.
- To realise that they cannot take responsibility for other people, and to let go when others want them to take over their problems for them.
- To feel good when they have accomplished something worthwhile.

Physical release

Scientists have long known how unresolved anger can lead to physical illness. So what better way to get rid of some of that anger than to release it in a constructive way? Lashing out at someone may feel good – albeit temporarily – because it releases some of that pent-up energy. But how can you keep that feel-good feeling without harming someone else?

Try some of these techniques to harness your energy in a constructive way:

- Go for a jog around the park.
- Take up a sport, such as football, kick-boxing or wrestling.
- Try aerobics.
- Hit a pillow.
- Scream it out – while you're alone.

Be aware that if you are not used to exercising, you may initially feel as if your anger is increasing when you begin. In reality, it's actually a surge of adrenaline which you are not used to.

Channel your emotions

If physical release isn't for you, there are many other ways to grab hold of your negative emotions and channel your anger into something more constructive. What works well for you might not appeal to others, so take these ideas with a pinch of salt:

- Get creative – make something that takes up all your energy and concentration.
- Listen to music – this can be at home, in a club or at a concert.
- Dance your heart out – your living room carpet will do nicely, or why not enrol in a ballroom dancing class?
- Take up a new hobby – bingo, horseriding, etc.

- Talk, talk and talk some more – find a helpful ear, either an anger buddy, a counsellor, your GP or just a caring friend. If you attend an anger management session, you can find out more about getting an anger buddy.

Thinking positively and believing in yourself

It goes without saying that the key to any type of self-improvement is to think positively and nurture your own feelings of self-esteem. It can be very difficult to make changes in your life if you are constantly beating yourself up for not being nicer, richer, stronger, more attractive, more intelligent – or less angry.

Learning how to successfully manage your anger is a process that can take time, and by reading this book you have already shown that you want to make the effort. Congratulate yourself for taking the first step towards making a real change in your life, and give yourself a break.

When things get difficult, realise that none of us are perfect and that you don't have to act perfectly all the time. When dealing with your anger, it's inevitable that you'll slip up from time to time. That's okay. The important thing is that when you do fall off the horse, you get right back on.

Putting thoughts into practice

It's important to keep telling yourself the importance of keeping your anger in control, and noticing how much better it feels to have healthy relationships with others which are not damaged by angry emotions.

Asserting yourself in a positive way is an incredibly empowering experience, and learning how to deal with others in that way can be both rewarding and enriching. Tell yourself that these feelings are not just a one-off, this new way of positive interaction feels good and should be how you want to continue for the rest of your life.

Gaining control of your life

If things get difficult, and they will, it's important to reiterate how much of a role anger plays in your life, and how nice it will be to get rid of it once and for all. Nobody ever said that anger management would be an easy process, but it's worth the effort.

Gaining control of your anger doesn't mean ignoring it completely and just hoping or wishing that it will go away. It means recognising your behaviour and learning to act on it or change it for the better. Only then can you gain control of your life.

'When you control your anger in very extreme circumstances, that is incredibly transformative and empowering as well.'

Mike Fisher, head of BAAM.

Looking towards the future

Keep in mind that while our past can help shape our present, it doesn't have to rule our future. Past events may have affected your life, but don't let them take over and have too much of an effect on what you are doing now.

Change is possible – people sometimes change almost beyond recognition! No matter what has happened or gone on before, it's never too late to make a change.

Staying on track

Depending on how serious your anger issues are, you will need to see your GP, who may recommend one of the following: self-help exercises, enrol in an anger management course or professional counselling.

'Recognise that every time you lose your cool, you give your power away every time your anger is inappropriately expressed. Every time you express your anger appropriately and respectfully, that is profoundly empowering,' says Mike Fisher, head of BAAM.

'When you control your anger in very extreme circumstances, that is incredibly transformative and empowering as well. When you are in a situation where you know you are going to lose it, then containing it is heroic. The more that people contain their anger and express themselves assertively, the more empowering it is for them.'

Summing Up

For anger management to work, it requires a real commitment, and by reading this book you have shown that you want to make a real change in your life. Whether you choose an anger management course, hypnosis, group or individual therapy, it is all up to you. The important thing is that you are taking charge of your life and doing something to change things for the better.

Learning how to keep your anger under control can have far-reaching effects on many aspects of your life, helping you to deal with people in an assertive, positive manner, and treating others with the respect they deserve. It can be life-affirming for you and will touch many other parts of your life, helping you to become happier and more productive in general.

You have now taken the first step towards becoming a happier person, one who is well-balanced and who can handle normal, everyday interaction on a calm and peaceful level. Congratulations! Keeping your anger in control requires hard work and determination, but you have shown you have the commitment needed to get there.

For more specific information on stress and depression, see *Stress – The Essential Guide* (Need2Know) and *Depression – The Essential Guide* (Need2Know).

Help List

British Association of Anger Management (BAAM)

Tel: 0845 1300 286
www.angermanage.co.uk
UK centre of expertise offering support, programmes and training for the general public. It provides individual and group support, workshops, training packages and seminars.

British Association for Behavioural and Cognitive Psychotherapies (BABCP)

Victoria Buildings, 9-13 Silver Street, Bury, BL9 OEU
Tel: 0161 797 2670
www.babcp.com
BABCP itself is the leading organisation for cognitive behaviour therapy in the UK, and can help people find therapists in their local area.

British Association for Counselling and Psychotherapy (BACP)

BACP House, 15 St John's Business Park, Lutterworth, LE17 4HB
Tel: 01455 883 316
bacp@bacp.co.uk
www.bacp.co.uk
A service enabling clients to find a suitable counsellor in their area.

British Association of Psychotherapists

37 Mapesbury Road, London, NW2 4HJ
Tel: 020 8452 9823
www.bap-psychotherapy.org
Offers psychoanalytic therapy to both children and adults, and can offer reduced fees for those on low incomes.

Centre for Stress Management

PO Box 26583, London, SE3 7EZ
Tel: 020 8318 4448
www.managingstress.com
Runs cognitive behavioural training programmes and offers executive, business, performance, stress and life coaching.

Childline

Tel: 0800 1111 (helpline, Monday to Sunday, 24-hour)
www.childline.org.uk
A helpline for children in the UK.

Everyman Project

1A Waterlow Road, London, N19 5NJ
Tel: 020 7263 8884 (helpline)
everyman@btopenworld.com
www.everymanproject.co.uk
Aims to help men change their angry, violent and/or abusive behaviour.

General Hypnotherapy Register

PO Box 204, Lymington, SO41 6WP
admin@general-hypnotherapy-register.com
www.general-hypnotherapy-register.com
Provides a register of qualified hypnotherapists.

Hampstead Hypnotherapy

Belsize Health, 16 England's Lane, London, NW3 4TG
Tel: 0207 419 2211
www.hampsteadhypnotherapy.com
Help with hypnosis to overcome all kinds of conditions and ailments which manifest either physically or emotionally e.g. weight loss, addictions, building confidence and anger management.

Institute of Family Therapy

24-32 Stephenson Way, London, NW1 2HX
Tel: 020 7391 9150
www.instituteoffamilytherapy.org.uk
Institute provides family therapy training for practitioners and counselling, therapy and mediation to families needing help.

International Stress Management Association UK (ISMA)

PO Box 491 Bradley, Stoke, Bristol, BS34 9AH
Tel: 0117 969 7284
stress@isma.org.uk
www.isma.org.uk
Organisation incorporating the charity that hosts national stress awareness day. The company promotes the prevention and reduction of stress.

Kidscape

2 Grosvenor Gardens, London, SW1W 0DH
Tel: 08451 205 204 (helpline, Monday to Friday, 10am-4pm)
Kidscape is committed to keeping children safe from abuse.

MIND

15-19 Broadway, Stratford, London, E15 4BQ
Tel: 0845 766 0163 (helpline, Monday to Friday, 9am-5pm)
www.mind.org.uk
Providing information and advice for people to take control of their mental health.

National Society for the Prevention of Cruelty to Children (NSPCC)

Tel: 0808 800 5000 (helpline, Monday to Sunday, 24-hour)
www.nspcc.org.uk
Children's charity devoted to wiping out child abuse.

Parentline Plus

Tel: 0808 800 2222 (helpline, Monday to Sunday, 24-hour)
www.parentlineplus.org.uk
National charity that works for, and with, parents.

Plymouth and District Mind

8 Woodside, Greenbank, Plymouth, PL4 8QE
Tel: 01752 254004
info@plymouthmind.org.uk
www.plymouthmind.org.uk
Runs a wide range of services for people who have mental health issues, including anger management classes.

Relate

Premier House, Carolina Court, Lakeside, Doncaster, DN4 5RA
Tel: 0300 100 1234
www.relate.org.uk
This well-known charity offers advice, relationship counselling, sex therapy, workshops, mediation, consultations and support. You can either meet with a counsellor face-to-face, by phone or through their website.

Samaritans

Chris, PO Box 9090, Stirling, FK8 2SA
Tel: 08457 90 90 90 (helpline, Monday to Sunday, 24-hour)
Tel: 1850 60 90 90 (helpline, Monday to Sunday, 24-hour, Republic of Ireland)
www.samaritans.org
Samaritans provides confidential non-judgemental emotional support, 24-hours a day for people who are experiencing feelings of distress or despair, including those which could lead to suicide.

SANE

1st Floor, Cityside House, 40 Adler Street London, E1 1EE
Tel: 0845 767 8000 (helpline, Monday to Sunday, 6pm-11pm)
sanemail@sane.org.uk
www.sane.org.uk

SANE is most famous for its national telephone line, which helps over 2,000 men, women and children every month who are affected by mental health issues.

United Kingdom Council for Psychotherapy (UKCP)

2nd Floor, Edward House, 2 Wakley Street, London, EC1V 7LT
Tel: 020 7014 9955
info@ukcp.org.uk
www.psychotherapy.org.uk
This is an umbrella organisation that has more than 80 training or accredited organisations under its membership.

Women's Aid (England)

Tel: 0808 200 0247 (helpline, Monday to Sunday, 24-hour)
www.womensaid.org.uk
Northern Ireland
Tel: 0800 917 1414 (helpline, Monday to Sunday, 24-hour)
www.niwaf.org
Scotland
Tel: 0800 027 1234 (helpline, Monday to Sunday, 24-hour)
www.scottishwomensaid.org.uk
Wales
Tel: 0808 801 0800 (helpline, Monday to Sunday, 24-hour)
www.welshwomensaid.org
National domestic violence charity working to end violence against women and children.

Young Minds

Tel: 0800 018 2138 (parent's helpline)
A charity dedicated to improving the emotional wellbeing and mental health of children and young people and empowering their parents and carers.

Need - 2 - Know

Available Titles Include ...

Allergies A Parent's Guide
ISBN 978-1-86144-064-8 £8.99

Autism A Parent's Guide
ISBN 978-1-86144-069-3 £8.99

Drugs A Parent's Guide
ISBN 978-1-86144-043-3 £8.99

Dyslexia and Other Learning Difficulties
A Parent's Guide ISBN 978-1-86144-042-6 £8.99

Bullying A Parent's Guide
ISBN 978-1-86144-044-0 £8.99

Epilepsy The Essential Guide
ISBN 978-1-86144-063-1 £8.99

Teenage Pregnancy The Essential Guide
ISBN 978-1-86144-046-4 £8.99

Gap Years The Essential Guide
ISBN 978-1-86144-079-2 £8.99

How to Pass Exams A Parent's Guide
ISBN 978-1-86144-047-1 £8.99

Child Obesity A Parent's Guide
ISBN 978-1-86144-049-5 £8.99

Applying to University The Essential Guide
ISBN 978-1-86144-052-5 £8.99

ADHD The Essential Guide
ISBN 978-1-86144-060-0 £8.99

Student Cookbook - Healthy Eating The Essential Guide
ISBN 978-1-86144-061-7 £8.99

Stress The Essential Guide
ISBN 978-1-86144-054-9 £8.99

Adoption and Fostering A Parent's Guide
ISBN 978-1-86144-056-3 £8.99

Special Educational Needs A Parent's Guide
ISBN 978-1-86144-057-0 £8.99

The Pill An Essential Guide
ISBN 978-1-86144-058-7 £8.99

University A Survival Guide
ISBN 978-1-86144-072-3 £8.99

Diabetes The Essential Guide
ISBN 978-1-86144-059-4 £8.99

View the full range at **www.need2knowbooks.co.uk**. To order our titles, call **01733 898103**, email **sales@n2kbooks.com** or visit the website.

Need - 2 - Know, Remus House, Coltsfoot Drive, Peterborough, PE2 9JX